First World War
and Army of Occupation
War Diary
France, Belgium and Germany

57 DIVISION
172 Infantry Brigade
King's (Liverpool Regiment)
2/9 Battalion
1 February 1917 - 31 January 1918

WO95/2985/4

The Naval & Military Press Ltd
www.nmarchive.com
Published in association with The National Archives

Published by

The Naval & Military Press Ltd

Unit 10 Ridgewood Industrial Park,

Uckfield, East Sussex,

TN22 5QE England

Tel: +44 (0) 1825 749494

www.naval-military-press.com

www.nmarchive.com

This diary has been reprinted in facsimile from the original. Any imperfections are inevitably reproduced and the quality may fall short of modern type and cartographic standards.

Contents

Document type	Place/Title	Date From	Date To
Heading	WO95/2985/4 57 Div. 172 Inf Brig 2/9 Kings Liverpool Regt 1917 Feb-1918 Jan		
War Diary	Blackdown	01/02/1917	16/02/1917
War Diary	Bois Grenier	04/02/1917	04/02/1917
War Diary	Grande Sec Bois	16/02/1917	16/02/1917
War Diary	Bailleul	21/02/1917	22/02/1917
War Diary	Outtersteene	21/02/1917	22/02/1917
War Diary	Estaires	23/02/1917	23/02/1917
War Diary	Erquinghem	25/02/1917	26/02/1917
Miscellaneous	2/9th Battalion "The King's' (Liverpool)	01/02/1917	01/02/1917
Map	Map		
War Diary		06/03/1917	28/03/1917
Miscellaneous	2/9th Battalion "The Kings 'S' (Lpool) Regiment	23/03/1917	23/03/1917
Miscellaneous	D.A.G. 3rd Echelon	03/05/1917	03/05/1917
War Diary	Erquinghem	28/03/1917	28/04/1917
Heading	War Diary Of 2/9th Battalion The King's (Liverpool Regiment) Period 1st May 1917 To 31st May 1917		
Miscellaneous	Headquarters 172nd Infantry Brigade	31/05/1917	31/05/1917
War Diary		01/05/1917	30/05/1917
Heading	War Diary Of 2/9th King's Liverpool Regiment From 1st June To 30 June 1917 (Volume 1)		
War Diary		01/06/1917	05/06/1917
War Diary	Flamengrie Sub Sector	03/06/1917	20/06/1917
Heading	War Diary Of 2/9th Battn "The Kings" (Liverpool) Regiment From 1/7/17 To 31/7/17 (Volume)		
War Diary		01/07/1917	31/07/1917
Heading	War Diary Of 2/9th Battalion "The King's" (Liverpool) Regiment From 1st August 1917 To 31st August 1917 Volume		
War Diary	Trenches Flamengrie Sector	01/08/1917	31/08/1917
Heading	War Diary Of The 2/9th Battalion "The King's" (Liverpool) Regt From 1st September 1917 To 30th September 1917 (Volume VIII)		
War Diary	Trenches Flamengrie Sub Sector	01/09/1917	04/09/1917
War Diary	In Brigade Reserve Bois Grenier Sector Near Erquinghem	05/09/1917	12/09/1917
War Diary	Flamengrie Sub Sector	13/09/1917	13/09/1917
War Diary	Bois Grenier Sector	13/09/1917	17/09/1917
War Diary	Village Of Sailly	18/09/1917	28/09/1917
War Diary	Honenghem	29/09/1917	30/09/1917
Heading	War Diary Of 2/9th Battalion "The King's" (Liverpool) Regt From 1st October 1917 To 31st October 1917 Volume		
War Diary	Honenghem	01/10/1917	19/10/1917
War Diary	Proven Area	20/10/1917	20/10/1917
War Diary	Refce Hazebruck 5a 1/100000 Area H.2	21/10/1917	25/10/1917
War Diary	Proven Area	26/10/1917	26/10/1917
War Diary	Malakoff Area	27/10/1917	27/10/1917
War Diary	Refce Sheet Belgium 28 N.W. Edition 6a 1/20,000 (B22b)	28/10/1917	31/10/1917

Heading	War Diary Of 2/9th Battalion "The King's" (Liverpool) Regiment From 1st November 1917 To 30th November 1917		
War Diary	Malakoff Area	01/11/1917	01/11/1917
War Diary	Schaap Balie	02/11/1917	04/11/1917
War Diary	Huddlestone Camp	05/11/1917	06/11/1917
War Diary	Refer Map Hazebruck 6a	07/11/1917	07/11/1917
War Diary	Nielles	08/11/1917	30/11/1917
Miscellaneous	List Of Salvage Brought Out Of The Line by 2/9th Battn. The Kings (Liverpool Regt) & Dumped At Huddleston Camp		
Heading	War Diary Of 2/9th Battalion "The King's" (Liverpool) Regt Period 1st December 1917 To 31st December 1917		
War Diary	Nielles	01/12/1917	07/12/1917
War Diary	Herzeele	08/12/1917	16/12/1917
War Diary	Emile Camp Elverdinghe	17/12/1917	24/12/1917
War Diary	Houthulst Forest	25/12/1917	29/12/1917
War Diary	Canal Bank	30/12/1917	31/12/1917
Miscellaneous	Relief Orders By Lieut. Col., E.V Manager Commandg "K" Battalion	26/12/1917	26/12/1917
Miscellaneous	Administrative Instructions	24/12/1917	24/12/1917
Operation(al) Order(s)	Operation Order No. 4 By Lieut. Col E.V. Manger Commanding "K" Battalion	24/12/1917	24/12/1917
Heading	War Diary Of 2/9th Battalion "The Kings" (Liverpool) Regt From 1/1/1918 To 31/1/1918		
War Diary	Canal Bank	01/01/1918	01/01/1918
War Diary	Boesinghe	02/01/1918	02/01/1918
War Diary	Dykes Camp	03/01/1918	04/01/1918
War Diary	Waterlands Camp	05/01/1918	12/01/1918
War Diary	L'Epinette Sub Sector	13/01/1918	18/01/1918
War Diary	Armentieres	19/01/1918	21/01/1918
War Diary	Waterlands	22/01/1918	27/01/1918
War Diary	Armentieres	28/01/1918	29/01/1918
War Diary	L'Epinnette Sub. Sector	30/01/1918	31/01/1918
Heading	57th Division 172nd Infy Bde 2-10th King's L'Pools 1915 Aug-1916 Feb And Feb 1917 July 1918		

WO 95 2985/4

57 Div, 172 Inf. Brig.

2/9 King's Liverpool Regt

1917 Feb – 1918 Jan

Instructions regarding War Diaries and Intelligence Summaries are contained in F. S. Regs., Part II. and the Staff Manual respectively. Title pages will be prepared in manuscript.

WAR DIARY
or
INTELLIGENCE SUMMARY.
(Erase heading not required.)

Army Form C. 2118.

2/9 Liverpool R.

Vol 1 2

Page I

Hour, Date, Place	Summary of Events and Information	Remarks and references to Appendices
1/2/17. Blackdown	The Battalion received Orders to prepare for embarkation and procedure was as follows	
1/2/17 do	Advance party	See APPENDIX I for Strength and Composition
15/2/17 do	Transport and details	
16/2/17 do	Main body	
4/2/17 BOIS GRENIER	The advance party proceeded via BOULOGNE and proceeded to Front line in the BOIS GRENIER Sector for instruction and reconnaissance and remained there until arrival of Battalion	
16/2/17 GRANDE SEC BOIS	The Transport and details disembarked at LE HAVRE detrained at BAILLEUL and proceeded to GRANDE SEC BOIS	

W4141—463. 400,000. 9/14. H.&J.Ltd. Forms/C. 2118/10.

Instructions regarding War Diaries and Intelligence Summaries are contained in F. S. Regs., Part II. and the Staff Manual respectively. Title pages will be prepared in manuscript.

WAR DIARY
or
~~INTELLIGENCE~~ SUMMARY.
(Erase heading not required.)

Army Form C. 2118.

Page II

Hour, Date, Place	Summary of Events and Information	Remarks and references to Appendices
	The Main body disembarked BOULOGNE and proceeded in 2 trains to BAILLEUL arriving as follows:-	
BAILLEUL 6PM 21/2/17	1st Train	
" 8AM 22/2/17	2nd Train	
21/2/17 OUTTERSTEENE	Billeted at OUTTERSTEENE	
22/2/17 "	Transport and details joined main body from GRANDE SEC BOIS	
23/2/17 ESTAIRES	Battalion proceeded by march route to ESTAIRES and billeted	
23/2/17 "	Advance party joined Battalion.	
23/2/17	The Battalion was completely concentrated - - - -	For details of personnel see Appendix II

Army Form C. 2118.

Instructions regarding War Diaries and Intelligence Summaries are contained in F. S. Regs., Part II. and the Staff Manual respectively. Title pages will be prepared in manuscript.

WAR DIARY
or
~~INTELLIGENCE SUMMARY.~~
(*Erase heading not required.*)

Hour, Date, Place	Summary of Events and Information	Remarks and references to Appendices
25/2/17 ERQUINGHEM	Battalion proceeded by march route to billets in ERQUINGHEM and relieved the 1st Battalion The CANTERBURY RIFLES 2nd NZ Inf Brigade 2nd A.N.Z.A Corps as divisional reserve in the BOIS-GRENIER Sector	
26/2/17 ERQUINGHEM	The relief of The 2nd NZ Inf Brigade being complete on this date The disposition of The 172 Inf Brigade in the sector was as follows:-	
	Right sub Sector — 2/10 Bn The Kings (L'pool) Regt Left " " — 2/4 Bn South Lancashire Regt Brigade reserve — 2/5 Bn South Lancashire Regt Divisional reserve — 2/9 Bn The Kings (L'Pool) Regt	See SKETCH MAP No 1. APPENDIX III

96

2/9th Battalion "THE KING'S" (Liverpool) Regt.

APPENDIX 1.

97/18

1st ADVANCE PARTY Proceeded 1/2/1917.

OFFICERS.	OTHER RANKS.
Capt. D.A.Wilson. " R.N.Mountfield. " G.F.Buckle. Lieut.H.E.Wigzell. 2/Lt. F.B.Clement. " L.T.Locan.	15.

= =

2nd ADVANCE PART. (TRANSPORT AND DETAILS)

OFFICERS.	OTHER RANKS.
MAJOR. S. RHODES. Lieut. A. Berry. Lieut A.G.Potter.	83.

HORSES.				VEHICLES.			
Offrs.	Riding	Draught.	Pack.	Wagons.	Carts.	M.Guns	bi-cycles
--	12.	46.	6.	18.	4	16.	9

= =

MAIN BODY.

OFFICERS	OTHER RANKS.
Lieut. Col. A.F.S.Leggatt. Major J.G.Paris. Capt. N.A.R.Van Gruisen. " H.H.Wilkinson. " H.M.Williams. " C. Myers. " A.S.Parkinson. R.A.M.C. " Rev. E. Fisher. C-E Lieut. & Adjt. J. Wright. " & Q.M. G.W.Crosbie. Lieut. P.H.Parker. " H.J.Hallett. " F.W.Veysey. " A.P.Candler. " A.E.Hunt. " W.Monks. 2/Lt. B.G.Povey. " F.W.Foster. " L. Walthew. " A.T.Barker. " J.W.Smith. " N.H.Sheard. " H.B.Briggs. " H.J.Spargo. " J.M.Parkes. " A.J.Harrison. " A. Roe. " ~~L.T.Locan.~~	856

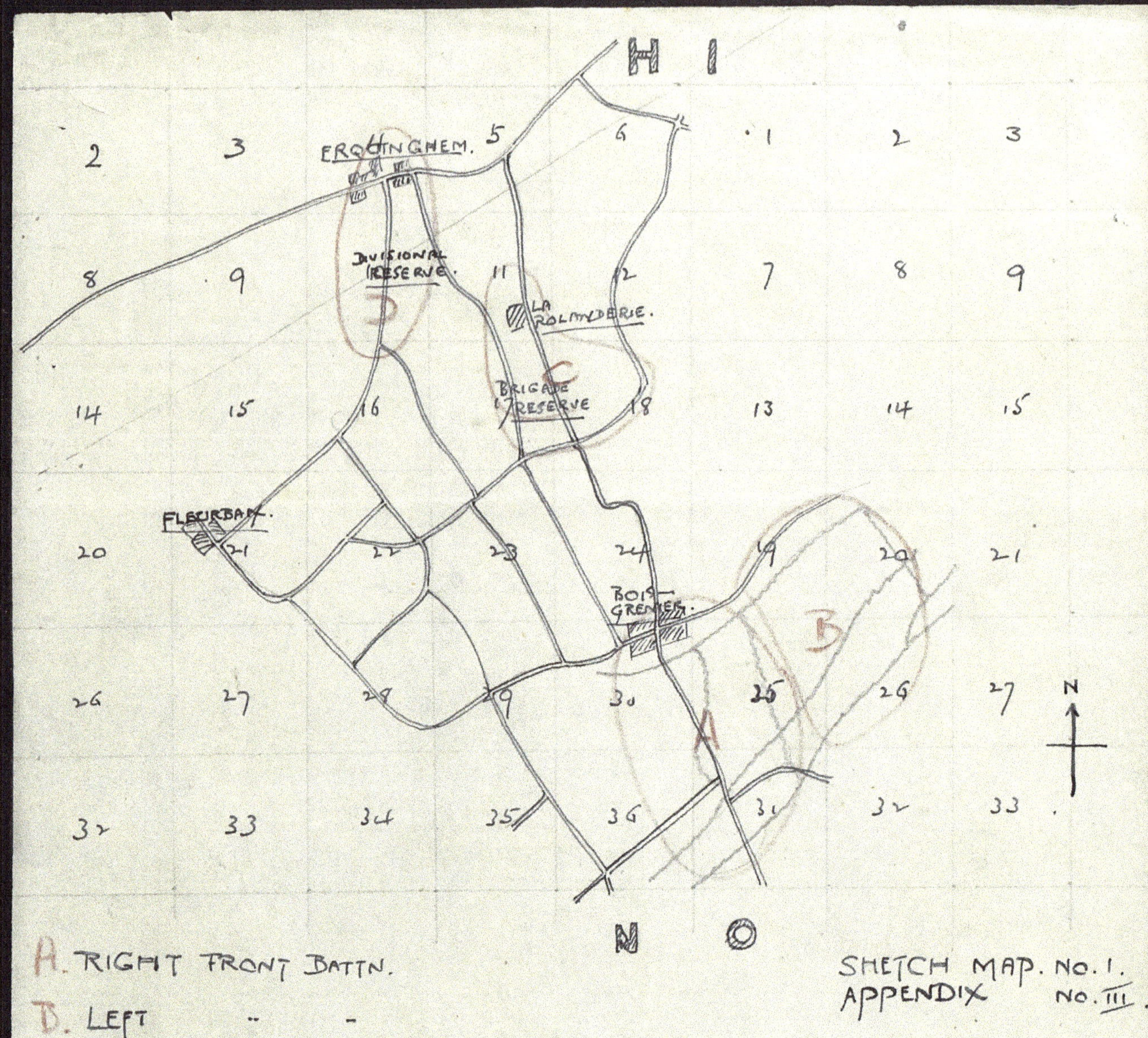

SKETCH MAP. NO. I.
APPENDIX NO. III.

A. RIGHT FRONT BATTN.
B. LEFT " "
C. BRIGADE RESERVE.
D. DIVISIONAL "

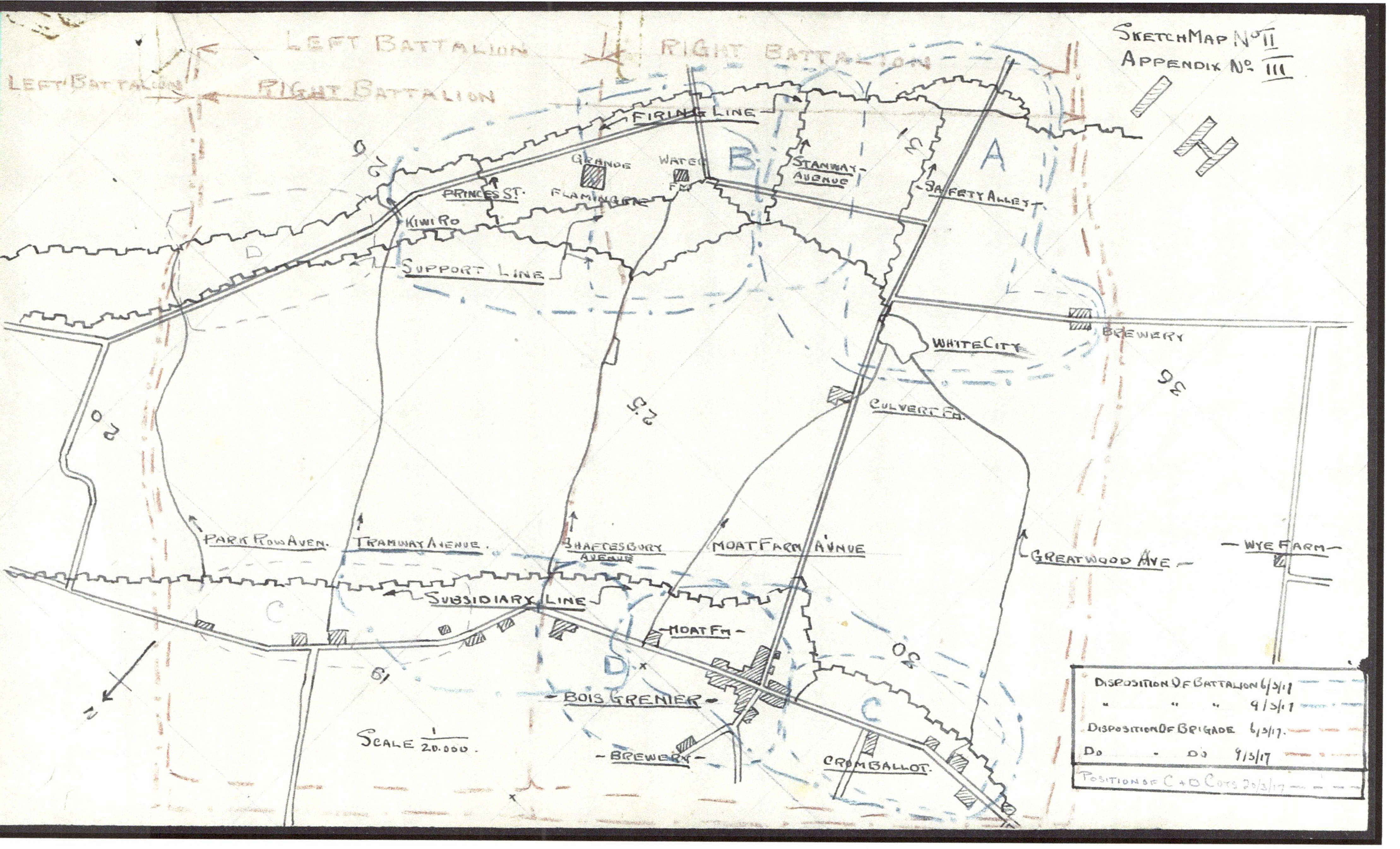

Sketch Map No. II
Appendix No. III
LEFT BATTALION
RIGHT BATTALION
LEFT BATTALION
RIGHT BATTALION
FIRING LINE
SUPPORT LINE
SUBSIDIARY LINE
PRINCES ST.
KIWI RD
STANWAY AVENUE
SAFETY ALLEY
WHITE CITY
BREWERY
CULVERT FM.
PARK ROW AVEN.
TRAMWAY AVENUE
SHAFTESBURY AVENUE
MOAT FARM AVNUE
GREATWOOD AVE
WYE FARM
MOAT FM
BOIS GRENIER
BREWERY
CROMBALLOT
Scale 1/20.000
N
Disposition of Battalion 6/3/17
" " " 9/3/17
Disposition of Brigade 6/3/17
Do - Do 9/3/17
Position of C + D Coys 20/3/17

57/72

2/9 Liverpool Rgt

Army Form C. 2118.

Instructions regarding War Diaries and Intelligence Summaries are contained in F. S. Regs., Part II. and the Staff Manual respectively. Title pages will be prepared in manuscript.

WAR DIARY
or
INTELLIGENCE SUMMARY.

(Erase heading not required.)

Hour, Date, Place	Summary of Events and Information	Remarks and references to Appendices
11 AM 6.3.17	The Battalion relieved 2/10 Bn Kings L'pool Regt in right sub sector one officer wounded during Relief X	X Lieut. P.H. Parker
	The sector of trenches was occupied by the battalion distributed as follows. A Coy Right Front line. Support line. B Coy Left " " " " C Right sector Subsidiary line D Left " " Bn Headquarters "THE RITZ"	See Sketch map No II Appendix III
9.3.17	The Battalion took over a larger frontage owing to a redistribution of the brigade frontage. Battalion headquarters moved to headquarters of left sub Section "THE CARLTON"	See Sketch map No II Appendix III
6-30 AM 14.3.17	The battalion was relieved by the 2/10 Bn Kings L'Pool Regt and moved into brigade reserve at LA ROLANDERIE less D Coy who remained in the Subsidiary line. During the period the Battalion was in the trenches the weather alternated between Frost and thaw and in consequence the trenches became in a very bad state	

2G

Instructions regarding War Diaries and Intelligence Summaries are contained in F. S. Regs., Part II. and the Staff Manual respectively. Title pages will be prepared in manuscript.

WAR DIARY
or
~~INTELLIGENCE~~ SUMMARY.
(Erase heading not required.)

Army Form C. 2118.

Hour, Date, Place	Summary of Events and Information	Remarks and references to Appendices
	no cases of Trench feet occurred and the health of the men remained good	
	Enemy artillery was fairly active during the whole period	
	Our artillery retaliated heavily and promptly on every occasion	
	Enemy MINNENWERFER very active but confined himself to one locality only	
	Enemy machine guns fairly active at nights	
	Enemy snipers entirely quiescent	
~~[illegible]~~	Casualties in battalion 2 OR Killed one Officer wounded (see above)	
18·3·17	C Company relieved D Company in subsidiary line	
20/3/17.	Relieved 2/10 Battalion KLR in BOIS GRENIER Sector.	
	disposition of Battalion as follows	
	Front line Right Company A Coy	See Sketch map No II appendix III
	" " Centre " B Coy	
	" " Left " D Coy	
	Subsidiary line " C Coy	
	Attached " one Company 2/10 KLR	

W4141—463. 400,000. 9/14. H.&J.Ltd. Forms/C. 2118/10.

Instructions regarding War Diaries and Intelligence Summaries are contained in F. S. Regs., Part II. and the Staff Manual respectively. Title pages will be prepared in manuscript.

WAR DIARY
or
~~INTELLIGENCE~~ SUMMARY.
(Erase heading not required.)

Army Form C. 2118.

Hour, Date, Place	Summary of Events and Information	Remarks and references to Appendices
28/3/17.	The Battalion was relieved by the 2/5 Kings Liverpool Regt and moved into Divisional reserve at ERQUINGHEM. The 172 Infantry Bde were relieved by the 17 Bde in the RUE DU BOIS and BOIS GRENIER Sectors and the whole of the 172 Inf Bde now in divisional reserve in the Vicinity of ERQUINGHEM. During the tour in the trenches the weather was on the whole good although 2 wet days occurred The health of the men remained good. No cases of trench foot. ~~Deaths~~ Casualties, Killed officers Nil Other Ranks Nil Wounded " Nil " " 6. Enemy artillery and Minnen-Werfer more active than during previous tour. Machine guns less active Snipers were absolutely quiet No enemy patrols were encountered by our patrols	

(73989) W4141—463. 400,000. 9/14. H.&J.Ltd. Forms/C. 2118/10.

Army Form C. 2118.

Instructions regarding War Diaries and Intelligence Summaries are contained in F. S. Regs., Part II. and the Staff Manual respectively. Title pages will be prepared in manuscript.

WAR DIARY
or
~~INTELLIGENCE~~ SUMMARY.
(*Erase heading not required.*)

Hour, Date, Place	Summary of Events and Information	Remarks and references to Appendices
	Our artillery active especially the Heavy Batteries who completed registering on and destroying works in rear of Enemy lines.	
	Medium and light T.M.B. carried out successful bombardments of Enemy front system and wire.	
	Patrols reconnoitred Enemy trenches and wire each night. The whole of No mans land also reconnoitred and in no cases were Enemy patrols encountered	

2/9th Battalion. "THE KING'S" (Lpool) Regiment.

APPENDIX 2.

DETAILS AS TO PERSONNEL etc. of BATTALION WHEN CONCENTRATED AT ESTAIRES 23/3/1917.

OFFICERS.		OTHER RANKS.
Lieut Col. A.F.S.Leggatt.	C.O.	
Major S. Rhodes.	2nd in command.	R.S.M. 7118 H. Binns
Major J.G.Paris	Div. Gas Sch.	
Lieut. & Adjt. J. Wright.		and 953 Other Ranks.
Hon.Lt. & Q.M. G.W.Crosbie.		
Capt. A.S.Parkinson.	M.O.	
Capt. E. Fisher. C.E.	Chaplain.	
Capt. C.Myers.	O.C."A" Coy.	
Capt. R.N.Mountfield.	"A" "	
2/Lieut. H.J.Spargo.	"A" "	
2/Lieut. L.T.Locan.	"A" "	
2/Lieut. L. Walthew.	"A" "	
2/Lieut. F. Foster.	"A" "	
2/Lieut. A.J.Harrison.	"A" "	
Capt. H.M.Williams.	O.C. "B" "	
Capt. D.A.Wilson.	"B" "	
Lieut. P.H.Parker.	"B" "	
Lieut. H J.Hallett.	"B" "	
Lieut. W. Monks.	"B" "	
Lieut. A. Berry.	"B" "	
2/Lieut. T.G.Povey.	"B" "	
2/Lieut. H.B.Briggs.	"B" "	
Capt. N.A.R.Van Gruisen.	O.C. "C" "	
Capt. G.F.Buckle.	"C" "	
Lieutenant. A.E.Hunt.	"C" "	
Lieut. H.E.Wigzell.	"C" "	
Lieut. F.W. Voysey.	"C" "	
2/Lieut. A.T.Barker.	"C" "	
2/Lieut. J.W.Smith.	"C" "	
2/Lieut. N.H.Sheard.	"C" "	
Capt. H.H.Wilkinson.	O.C. "D" "	
Capt. J.A.Mair.	"D" "	
Lieut. A.G.Potter.	"D" "	
Lieut. A.P.Candler.	"D" "	
2/Lieut. F.B.Clement.	"D" "	
2/Lieut. J.M.Parkes.	"D" "	
2/Lieut. A. Roe.	"D" "	

DETAILS OF TRANSPORT.

ANIMALS.

HORSES				MULES	
Riding	Draught	Heavy Draught	Pack	Large	Small.
12	6	9	7	-	22

GUNS, LIMBERS, TRANSPORT VEHICLES ETC.

Machine Guns	Horsed 4 Wheeled	Horsed 2 Wheeled	BICYCLES.
16	14	4	9

D.A.G.
3rd ECHELON.

Herewith War Diary of this unit for month ending 30th April 1917.

3/8/17.

Major
2/9th Bn. King's Lpool Regt.

2/9 Liverpool R 57

Vol 3

Army Form C. 2118.

Instructions regarding War Diaries and Intelligence Summaries are contained in F. S. Regs., Part II. and the Staff Manual respectively. Title pages will be prepared in manuscript.

WAR DIARY or INTELLIGENCE SUMMARY.

(Erase heading not required.)

Hour, Date, Place	Summary of Events and Information	Remarks and references to Appendices
28/3/17 to 12/4/17. ERQUINGHEM	The Battalion remained in divisional reserve at ERQUINGHEM. Strength of Battalion 31/3/17 as per margin. During this period 15 platoons were employed daily under the CRE for work on the subsidiary or rear lines of the divisional area. CASUALTIES during period of Work. Owing to this it was only possible for the battalion to undergo a limited amount of training mainly confined to training of platoon ergts. Bombers and Lewis gunners with the object of creating a staff of instructors in the above subjects.	Strength of unit: 36 Officers, 918 Other ranks. Fighting Strength: 28 Officers, 775 Other ranks. 4. O R Wounded.
	On the night of 10/4/17 a Raid was carried out by about 90 officers and men of the 172 inf Bde the number of O Ranks of this Battalion participating were 22. The raid was carried out with the object of obtaining identification of enemy units + reconnaissance of enemy dispositions. The raid met strong enemy opposition and did not succeed in entering enemy trench. Casualties sustained by NCOs and men of this battalion participating in the raid are shewn in the margin	Casualties: Killed 330652 Sergt R PIERCE. MISSING 331273 Pte R BODELL, 331195 Pte F VINING. Wounded 1 Corporal, 3. Privates

(73989) W4141—463. 400,000. 9/14. H.&J.Ltd. Forms/C. 2118/10.

Instructions regarding War Diaries and Intelligence Summaries are contained in F. S. Regs., Part II. and the Staff Manual respectively. Title pages will be prepared in manuscript.

WAR DIARY
or
~~INTELLIGENCE~~ SUMMARY.

(*Erase heading not required.*)

Army Form C. 2118.

Hour, Date, Place	Summary of Events and Information	Remarks and references to Appendices
12/4/17	The 172 Inf Brigade relieved 171 Inf Bde in the BOIS GRENIER and RUE-du BOIS Sectors.	Map Reference Sheet 36 Scale 1/20000
	The Battalion less A Coy relieved 2/5 Kings Liverpool Regt in Brigade reserve at LA ROLANDRIE H 17 B 1 9	2/Lieut F Fisher joined for duty 18/4/17 from 7th (Res) KLR and was posted to "B" Coy
	"A" Company proceeded to the BOIS GRENIER Sector and took up position in the SUBSIDIARY LINE in support of the 2/10 KLR.	
	Disposition of 172 Inf Bde on this date as follows	
	BOIS GRENIER SECTOR Front line 2/10 KLR. Reserve 2/9 KLR	
	RUE DU BOIS SECTOR Front line 2/4 S Lancs Regt Reserve 2/5 S Lancs Regt	
16/4/17	B Coy relieved A Coy in subsidiary line	
20/4/17	The Battalion relieved the 2/10 KLR in the BOIS GRENIER Sector and occupied the trenches in the following order	
	Right front Company C	
	Centre " " A	
	Left " " D	
	Subsidiary line Company B	
	Attached 1 Coy 2/10 KLR in Subsidiary line	
	Relief completed without Casualties.	

(73989) W4141—463. 400,000. 9/14. H.&J.Ltd. Forms/C. 2118/10.

Instructions regarding War Diaries and Intelligence Summaries are contained in F. S. Regs., Part II. and the Staff Manual respectively. Title pages will be prepared in manuscript.

WAR DIARY
or
~~INTELLIGENCE SUMMARY.~~
(Erase heading not required.)

Army Form C. 2118.

Hour, Date, Place	Summary of Events and Information	Remarks and references to Appendices
24/4/17 11 AM	Hostile Aeroplane brought down by M Gun fire from one of our planes in No Mans Land opposite Centre Company	
25/4/17 11 PM	Patrol under 2/Lt L.T. Logan reconnoitred plane they brought in to our lines portions of the Machine remains of Photographic apparatus etc. The Pilot was completely incinerated and no identification was obtained	
25/6-4-17	On this night patrol under 2/Lt. A T Barker penetrated first line of enemy system with the object of obtaining hostile identification the patrol was absent from our lines 3½ hours but did not succeed in their object. The attempt was repeated on the night 27/8-4-17 but no results were obtained altho patrol penetrated a similar distance	
28/4/17	The Battalion was relieved by 2/10 Liverpool Regt and moved into Brigade Reserve at LA ROLANDERIE less D Coy which remained in the subsidiary line in support of the 2/10 Liverpool Regt. During the period spent in the trenches the enemy showed more activity than usual. His artillery was very active during the whole period BOIS GRENIER and the houses and farms in the vicinity were subjected to heavy shelling by artillery of all Calibres	

Instructions regarding War Diaries and Intelligence Summaries are contained in F. S. Regs., Part II. and the Staff Manual respectively. Title pages will be prepared in manuscript.

WAR DIARY
or
~~INTELLIGENCE SUMMARY.~~
(Erase heading not required.)

Army Form C. 2118.

Hour, Date, Place	Summary of Events and Information	Remarks and references to Appendices
	The use of rifle grenades and light trench mortars firing PINEAPPLE bombs by the enemy was very marked during the period.	
	Enemy patrols and snipers were wholly inactive during the period in the trenches.	
	On the night 28/4/17 The enemy heavily shelled the sector during the relief. The relief was successfully carried out with only one casualty.	Casualties officers 2Lt. A.P. Candler (accidentally wounded)
	Our light and medium trench mortars carried out successful bombardments of enemy wire and front line trenches during the period.	Casualties. other Ranks
	Our Field Artillery replied promptly to calls for retaliation on each occasion when called for.	10 Wounded.
	Heavy artillery registered and carried out destructive fire on rear works of the enemy	1. Accidentally wounded

(73989) W4141—463. 400,000. 9/14. H.&J.Ltd. Forms/C. 2118/10.

4 G

Vol 4

War Diary

of

2/9th Battalion The King's (Liverpool Regiment)

Period

1st May 1917 to 31st May 1917.

In the Field.
1st June 1917.

Headquarters,
172nd Infantry Brigade.

Herewith War Diary for this Battalion for period 1st to 31st May incl.

31/5/17.

Major
Commdg. 2/9th Bn. King's Lpool. Regt.

Instructions regarding War Diaries and Intelligence Summaries are contained in F. S. Regs., Part II. and the Staff Manual respectively. Title pages will be prepared in manuscript.

WAR DIARY
or
INTELLIGENCE SUMMARY.
(Erase heading not required.)

Army Form C. 2118.

Hour, Date, Place	Summary of Events and Information	Remarks and references to Appendices
4/5/17	Capt G. C. Williams R.A.M.C.(T) 2/3 Wessex F.A. attached for duty vice Capt. A. S. Parkinson	Casualties. 1 o/r wounded. 4/5/17
6/5/17	The Battalion (less 1 Coy) relieved 7/10 Kings (Liverpool) Regiment in BOIS. GRENIER SUBSECTOR. C Coy being in subsidiary line.	1 " " 5/5/17 1 " " 6/5/17
7/5/17	Gun positions in ERQUINGHEM-LYS shelled heavily from 10.0 am to 2.0 pm.	Refer Trench map, BOIS-GRENIER 36 NW. 4 edition 7a. 1:10000
	A Gas Alarm was received from Battalion on our left but our subsector was not affected.	
7/5/17	At 10.10 pm enemy put a box barrage on our front and support lines I 31.1 - I 31.4. SAFETY ALLEY, STANWAY AVE. EMMA POST, BIRDCAGE WALK and WHITE CITY. Our artillery retaliated. Enemy ceased fire 10.40 pm. Working party of the Battalion was at work in the front line in SALIENT LOCALITY and suffered fairly heavy casualties. For our casualties see margin.	
8/5/17	BOIS-GRENIER shelled	8/5/17 1 o/r wounded

(73989) W4141—463. 400,000. 9/14. H.&J.Ltd. Forms/C. 2118/10.

Instructions regarding War Diaries and Intelligence Summaries are contained in F. S. Regs., Part II. and the Staff Manual respectively. Title pages will be prepared in manuscript.

WAR DIARY
or
INTELLIGENCE SUMMARY.
(Erase heading not required.)

Army Form C. 2118.

Hour, Date, Place	Summary of Events and Information	Remarks and references to Appendices
9-10/5/17	A special raiding party of 2 Sgts and 12 o/r crossed enemy's wire at I 26 d. 1 4 and lay up against his front line parapet for 1¼ hours. No enemy passed along the trench.	Casualties 5 o/r wounded
11/5/17.	ERQUINGHEM-LYS again shelled.	1 off. (Lt [illegible]) 1 o/r wounded 11/5/17
10.30 pm.	Enemy fired a large number of gas shells from 2 guns. Effect very local and momentary. Shells fell to [illegible] of gap (I 31 [illegible])	
12 May	A special patrol endeavoured to raid enemy's trenches at point I 26 d 25 60 but after getting through his wire patrol found borrow ditch 12 to 16 ft wide which could not be crossed without a bridge.	[illegible] wounded [illegible] duty [illegible]/17
12-13/5/17.	A raiding party of 2 officers and 26 o/r with two covering parties entered enemy's front line at I 26 b. ~~65.20~~ 8 3 at 11.55 pm. Attacking party crossed to INCOMPLETE SUPPORT however prevented from entering by a borrow ditch. Party remained in enemy's lines for 1½ hrs but did not encounter the enemy.	1 o/r wounded [illegible]/17
13/5/17	GRIS POT battery shelled between 8.0 am and 12.0 noon.	1 o/r wounded [illegible]/17

(73989) W4141—463. 400,000. 9/14. H.&J.Ltd. Forms/C. 2118/10.

Instructions regarding War Diaries and Intelligence Summaries are contained in F. S. Regs., Part II. and the Staff Manual respectively. Title pages will be prepared in manuscript.

WAR DIARY
or
INTELLIGENCE SUMMARY.
(*Erase heading not required.*)

Army Form C. 2118.

Hour, Date, Place	Summary of Events and Information	Remarks and references to Appendices
14/5/17	The Battalion less A Company, remaining in Subsidiary Line, was relieved by 2/10 Bn. Kings L'pool Regt. and proceeded to billets at LA ROLANDERIE (B.H.Q.) LA ROLANDERIE FARM (C. D Companies) Huts near STREAKY BACON FARM. (B. Coy.) During the tour in the trenches enemy's artillery has been very active at times. He has also used his heavy trench mortars again after a period of inactivity, his principal target being area O.15	Casualties 1 o/r wounded (accidentally) 7/5/17
15/5/17	A Coy relieved by B Coy. (Subsidiary Line)	
	Name of SUBSECTOR occupied by Battn altered to "FLAMENGRIE" Centre Rde Sector now known as BOIS-GRENIER Sector.	1 o/r wounded 20/5/17. 2/Lt A. Lamont joined the Bn for duty 21/5/17 from 3/9 KLR
22/5/17	The Battalion relieved 2/10 Bn. Kings L'pool Regt in FLAMENGRIE subsector.	1 o/r Killed 24/5/17.
25-6/5/17	At 1.30 am 26/5/17 a fighting patrol of 2 officers and 38 o/r (2/10 KLR) left our line at point I 32 a 04.75 with the intention of entering the enemy's trenches about I 32 a 50.35 but when about 50 yds from his wire the enemy opened fire with 3 machine guns and patrol was forced to return having suffered severe casualties (2 Killed 9 wounded)	

Instructions regarding War Diaries and Intelligence Summaries are contained in F. S. Regs., Part II. and the Staff Manual respectively. Title pages will be prepared in manuscript.

WAR DIARY
or
INTELLIGENCE SUMMARY.
(Erase heading not required.)

Army Form C. 2118.

Hour, Date, Place	Summary of Events and Information	Remarks and references to Appendices
25-6/5/17 (cont^d)	Previous to this enterprise (11.5 pm. 27/5/17) 150 Gas projectors were fired simultaneously on front and support lines (INCONSISTENT)	Casualties.
27/5/17 3 am	Enemy fired large number of gas shells into COLLEGE GN locality	
28-9/5/17	Listening post in front of C.P. I 26 1 heard enemy patrol approaching. The enemy must have seen or heard our post as he retired immediately.	13 o/r wounded 28/5/17 (including 7 suffering from effects of gas and 1 at duty)
29-30/5/17	Battle patrol 2/Lt A.T. Barker [illegible] saw enemy [illegible] party of about 20 men advancing. When about 30 yards away our patrol attacked ([illegible]) [illegible] one round was fired by each man and [illegible] Lewis [illegible] inflicted on enemy [illegible] with bayonets. The enemy fled to his line [illegible] followed by our patrol. One wounded prisoner was brought in [illegible] identification. We sustained no casualties.	2 o/r wounded 29/5/17 (1 accidentally)
30/5/17	The battalion, less D Coy. remaining in Subsidiary line, were relieved by 2/10 K.L.R. and went into billets near ERQUINGHEM-LYS.	

(T-989) W4141—463. 400,000. 9/14. H.&J.Ltd. Forms/C. 2118/10.

Instructions regarding War Diaries and Intelligence Summaries are contained in F. S. Regs., Part II. and the Staff Manual respectively. Title Pages will be prepared in manuscript.

WAR DIARY
or
INTELLIGENCE SUMMARY
(Erase heading not required.)

Army Form C. 2118

Place	Date	Hour	Summary of Events and Information	Remarks and references to Appendices
	30/5/17 (cont^d)		B. H. Q. I 17 d 4.3 A Coy } LA ROLANDERIE FME. B C Huts near "STREAKY BACON FARM." During period in trenches our artillery were very enterprising and aggressive. Enemy's artillery very quiet. He seemed to have withdrawn the majority of his guns and relied on increased T.M. activity. 'Rum Jars' & Heavy T.M. were frequently employed against C.T.s several of which were heard temporarily out of use. Some dug outs and firebays were wrecked, 'Hows' retaliated with good effect; one H.T.M. was moved to an alternative position. A large number of 'Pineapples' were fired into SALIENT Locality (I. 31.) throughout the tour, often at night in reply to L.G. fire. Enemy has made obvious repairs to his parapet in INCREASE and INDEX trenches. More noise than usual has been heard in enemy's lines during night.	

1875 Wt. W593/826 1,000,000 4/15 J.B.C. & A. A.D.S.S./Forms/C. 2118.

5 G

Vol 5

Confidential

War Diary
of
2/9th Kings Liverpool Regiment.
From 1st June to 30 June 1917.
(Volume 1)

Army Form C. 2118

Instructions regarding War Diaries and Intelligence Summaries are contained in F. S. Regs., Part II. and the Staff Manual respectively. Title Pages will be prepared in manuscript.

WAR DIARY

~~or~~

~~INTELLIGENCE SUMMARY~~

(Erase heading not required.)

Place	Date	Hour	Summary of Events and Information	Remarks and references to Appendices
	1/6/17		The following letter of congratulation has been received with reference to the gas shell attack made on the Battn on the morning of the 27th May. "The Divisional Commander congratulates the 2/9th Kings Liverpool Reg. on the very few casualties they had during the early morning of the 27th May from the enemy gas shell attack. The attack was one of some severity, and the promptitude with which Box respirators were put on, and the local alarm given reflects great credit on all concerned." [illegible initials]	

1875 Wt. W593/826 1,000,000 4/15 J.B.C. & A. A.D.S.S./Forms/C. 2118.

Army Form C. 2118

Instructions regarding War Diaries and Intelligence Summaries are contained in F. S. Regs., Part II. and the Staff Manual respectively. Title Pages will be prepared in manuscript.

WAR DIARY

~~or~~

~~INTELLIGENCE SUMMARY~~

(Erase heading not required.)

Place	Date	Hour	Summary of Events and Information	Remarks and references to Appendices
	5/6/17		The following letters of congratulation have been received in reference to the listening patrol under 2nd Lieut Barker:- (1) "Corps Commander wishes his congratulations conveyed to Colonel Leggatt Commanding "K" Battn on the enterprise and spirit shown by 2nd Lieut Barker and the men who attacked hostile party in No Man's land on morning of May 30th. and who captured a prisoner." A.P. (2) "The G O C. Division congratulates the 2/9th Liverpool Regiment on the action of the listening Patrol commanded by 2nd Lieut Barker on the night of 29/30th May. The promptitude of their action, and the dash displayed, is highly creditable. A.P. (3) "The G O C Brigade wishes to congratulate 2nd Lt. Barker and the patrol of K Battn. on winning the Brigade competition. This patrol attacked a German Patrol three times its strength with the bayonet, and chased the Germans back to their own lines, obtaining one prisoner and wounding others. The G. O. C hopes that other patrols will adopt the same Tactics and show the same excellent spirit." A.P.	

1875 Wt. W593/826 1.000.000 4/15 J.B.C. & A. A.D.S.S./Forms/C. 2118.

Instructions regarding War Diaries and Intelligence Summaries are contained in F. S. Regs., Part II. and the Staff Manual respectively. Title Pages will be prepared in manuscript.

WAR DIARY ~~or~~ ~~INTELLIGENCE SUMMARY~~

(Erase heading not required.)

Army Form C. 2118

Place	Date	Hour	Summary of Events and Information	Remarks and references to Appendices
FLAMENGRIE SUBSECTOR.	3/6/17		'D' Coy (fifth company) in Subsidiary Line were relieved by "C" Coy. MB	
	7/6/17		The Battalion relieved 7/10th Bn. "The Kings" (L'pool) Regt., relief being completed at 11.50 P.M. During the period of rest there were no unusual occurrences. The area occupied was not shelled. The Gazette dated 5/6/17 deprived a number of officers of their temporary rank, leaving the Battn: without a single Captain. MB	
	10-11/6/17.		A party consisting of 2 Officers and 36 O/R went out with the intention of making a Silent Raid of the enemy's lines, to inflict casualties upon him, obtaining identification and ascertain the strength of his front line garrison. On arriving at his Trenches the party found the enemy occupying them in force. A sharp encounter followed when several of the enemy were Killed and wounded. In spite of a barrage of trench mortars our party lost one man (missing) returned to our lines, the casualties sustained being 4 men slightly wounded. The commanding officer Lt. Col. A J A Leggett whilst attending operations from the Breastwork was slightly wounded. MB	
	11/12 and 12/13 June 1917.		Parties consisting of 1 N.C.O. and 2 O/R went out and occupied a shell-hole about 15 yards from enemy's front line breastwork for 24 hours. Neither party was discovered. Valuable local information was obtained. MB	

1875 Wt. W593/826 1,000,000 4/15 J.B.C. & A. A.D.S.S./Forms/C. 2118.

Instructions regarding War Diaries and Intelligence Summaries are contained in F. S. Regs., Part II. and the Staff Manual respectively. Title Pages will be prepared in manuscript.

WAR DIARY

~~or~~

~~INTELLIGENCE SUMMARY~~

(Erase heading not required.)

Army Form C. 2118

Place	Date	Hour	Summary of Events and Information	Remarks and references to Appendices
FLAMENGRIE SUBSECTOR.	14/6/17.		The Battalion was relieved by 12th PORTUGUESE Battalion. The relief was carried out successfully and was completed by 10.0 pm.	
			The Battalion went into billets at ERQUINGHEM-LYS. AB	
			During the tour of the trenches a marked change was noticed in the enemy's operations, indicating a relief or an alteration in his defences and tactics which may have been due to our activity North of this subsector (MESSINES and PLOEGSTEERT). He has been more active by day – with artillery and Trench Mortars, Snipers, &c, and more alert at night. AB	
			Information having been received that a withdrawal of the enemy was possible our activity in raiding and patrolling was increased but no information regarding an enemy retirement was obtained: his trenches were being held strongly. AB	
			Our artillery has been active and effective retaliation has been forthcoming when required.	
			Hostile Artillery and Trench Mortar activity has been directed chiefly against our left flank, the trenches opposite which are less strongly held than opposite our right.	
			Only one hostile patrol reported (11/12th)	
			AB.	

1875 Wt. W593/826 1.000.000 4/15 J.B.C. & A. A.D.S.S./Forms/C. 2118.

Army Form C. 2118

Instructions regarding War Diaries and Intelligence Summaries are contained in F. S. Regs., Part II. and the Staff Manual respectively. Title Pages will be prepared in manuscript.

WAR DIARY

or

~~INTELLIGENCE SUMMARY~~

(Erase heading not required.)

Place	Date	Hour	Summary of Events and Information	Remarks and references to Appendices
			AWARD.	
	10/6/17		Under authority granted by H.M. The King, the Field Marshal Commanding-in-Chief has awarded the MILITARY CROSS to the undermentioned Officer for gallantry and devotion to duty in action:-	
			SEC. LIEUT. A. T. BARKER. 7th Btn K.L.R. (T.F.)	
			CASUALTIES. Offrs. — O/R.	
	31/5/17		— 1 wounded	
	4/6/17		— 1 "	
	5/6/17		— 2	
	9/6/17		1 — 2 " (2/Lt. A.E. HUNT)	
	11/6/17		1 — 3 " (Lt Col. A P S LEGGATT)	
	14/6/17		— 8 1 killed, 6 wounded, 1 missing	
	14/6/17		1. — 1 wounded (2/Lt A.J. HARRISON)	
	14/6/17		On being relieved the Battalion went into Billets at ERQUINGHEM for 6 days for rest.	
	20/6/17		On completion of which time we relieved the 10th (Scottish) K.L.R. in Brigade Reserve. Less A Co who relieved a company of the Scottish in Subsidiary line of Flamengrie subsector. The remainder of the month was passed in Brigade Reserve, with the exception of C Company who went into the line on the night of the 27th, & D Company who relieved A on the 28th. The two other companies & all other available men were employed on working parties during the nights of 26th, 27th & 28th.	
			[illegible] Major 30/6/17	

1875 Wt. W593/826 1,000,000 4/15 J.B.C. & A. A.D.S.S./Forms/C. 2118.

6G

Confidential.

War Diary

of

2/9th Battn "The Kings" (Liverpool) Regiment

From:- 1/7/17. To:- 31/7/17.

(Volume.......).

Instructions regarding War Diaries and Intelligence Summaries are contained in F. S. Regs., Part II. and the Staff Manual respectively. Title Pages will be prepared in manuscript.

WAR DIARY
or
INTELLIGENCE SUMMARY
(Erase heading not required.)

Army Form C. 2118

Place	Date	Hour	Summary of Events and Information	Remarks and references to Appendices
	1-7-17 to 8-7-17		The Battalion remained in Brigade reserve less B & C Companies who remained in the Trenches until the 4th inst. on which date C Company was relieved by D. Co.	
	9/7/17.		The remainder of the Battalion joined B & D Companies in the Trenches & relieved The 2/10th Scottish Bn K.L.R. in the Flamengrie Subsector. Disposition of the line. right subsector C. Co. centre " A Co. Left " D Co. Subsidiary line. B Co.	
	10/7/17.		A Patrol of 1 officer & 4 O.R. reconnoitred the ground in N.M.L. on their right in view of future operations, & detected enemies listening Post.	
	11/7/17		Our T.M.Bs. active on to enemies wire & support Trenches. which brought back heavy retaliation. A Patrol of 1 officer & 8 O.R. went out from right subsector with a view to capturing enemy listening Post heard the previous night.	
	12/7/17.		Same Patrol as on previous two nights was out in front of our right subsector. Patrol of 1 N.C.O. & four men patrolled in front of left subsector, & located an enemy listening Post but owing to the fact that the enemy held a position at a Bridge on their side of a wide Ditch surprise was impossible.	
	13/7/17.		Same Patrol on the right subsector, & Post was again located, unfortunately however our artillery fired on to Trench behind listening Post, & the enemy retired without our Patrol being able to cut them off. A Patrol of 1 officer & 15 men went out on the left to cut off listening Post detected the previous night, but no enemy were encountered.	

C. C. Thin Major

1875 Wt. W593/826 1,000,000 4/15 J.B.C. & A. A.D.S.S./Forms/C. 2118.

Instructions regarding War Diaries and Intelligence Summaries are contained in F. S. Regs., Part II. and the Staff Manual respectively. Title Pages will be prepared in manuscript.

WAR DIARY
or
INTELLIGENCE SUMMARY
(Erase heading not required.)

Army Form C. 2118

Place	Date	Hour	Summary of Events and Information	Remarks and references to Appendices
	14/7/17 to 17/7/17		Patrol out on night as on previous nights but no contact gained with the enemy. T M B shoots in conjunction with our Artillery took place daily. With the exception of retaliation to our Artillery & T M B shoots which took place daily, there was a very quiet time in the Trenches. The 2/5th South Lancs Reg relieved the Batt on the evening of the 17th with the exception of A Co who remained in as fifth Company. The Battalion returned to Billets in Brigade Reserve around ERQUINGHEM	
	21/7/17		D Company relieved A Company in Subsidiary line of Trenches	
	25/7/17		The Battalion relieved the 2/5 South Lancs Reg on the night of the 25th inst in the Flamengrie subsection	
	24/7/17		Captain J Mair took over command of A Company from Captain R W Mountfield	
	21/7/17		During the day from 6 30 am The Trenches were subjected to a very heavy Bombardment from Trench Mortars until 5 30 pm. considerable damage was done to the Trenches, the support line suffering the most heavily	
	2[illegible]/7/17		A Patrol of 1 NCO & 4 men went out & examined enemy wire after T M B shoot in front of [illegible] Trench. A Patrol of 1 NCO & 3 men also examined wire after T M B shoot in front of [illegible] Trench	
	26/7/17		enemy very active from 6 pm to 11 30 pm with his artillery & T M B's	
	27/7/17		A quiet day enemy retaliated to our T M B shoot to a small extent. A Patrol of 1 NCO & 3 men entered enemy Trench called [illegible] & lay in wait for the enemy, but none encountered	

1875 Wt. W593/826 1,000,000 4/15 J.B.C. & A. A.D.S.S./Forms/C. 2118.

C. S. Thompson Major

Instructions regarding War Diaries and Intelligence Summaries are contained in F. S. Regs., Part II. and the Staff Manual respectively. Title Pages will be prepared in manuscript.

WAR DIARY
or
INTELLIGENCE SUMMARY
(Erase heading not required.)

Army Form C. 2118

Place	Date	Hour	Summary of Events and Information	Remarks and references to Appendices
	27/28		A Patrol of 1 NCO & 4 men reconnoitred wire in front of Increase Trench. The Battalion on our left was subjected to a heavy gas shell Bombardment but noone was affected in the 2/9th.	
	28th		A quiet day. enemy putting a few shells to the right of College Green Willow Avenue.	
	28/29th		A Patrol of one officer & 10 men with Lewis gun went out with the object of capturing suspected enemy listening Post. which however was found unoccupied. A Party of 5 OR then proceeded into enemy Trench at INDEX which was found to be unoccupied	
	29th		Our Artillery in cooperation with the TMB's bombarded enemy Trenches in the morning & afternoon. enemy retaliated with 100 shells on to support line from which our men had previously been withdrawn	
	30th		Our Artillery active all day shelling enemy back areas & enemy Trenches. very little retaliation from enemy in consideration of the large amount of shells fired at him. about 90-100 shells being received & 20 Sneapples	
	30/31st		A Patrol of 1 NCO & 4 men went out to examine wire after TMB shoot but owing to number of very lights being sent up, they were unable to make the reconnaissance. They returned to our lines, & after strengthening the party with an additional four men, the work was successfully carried out.	
	8th		Lt Col A. F. S. Leggatt went to Hospital on the 8th rejoining on the 16th during which time Major E. G. THIN took over the command.	
	28th		Lt Col A. F. S. Leggatt gave up the command of the Battalion on the 28th inst. Major E. G. THIN taking over temporary command.	

E. G. Thin
Major

1875 Wt. W593/826 1,000,000 4/15 J.B.C. & A. A.D.S.S./Forms/C. 2118.

Vol 7 7.G

Confidential.

War Diary

of

2/9th Battalion "The King's" (Liverpool) Regiment.

From 1st August 1917 To 31st August 1917.

Volume ....

Instructions regarding War Diaries and Intelligence Summaries are contained in F. S. Regs., Part II. and the Staff Manual respectively. Title Pages will be prepared in manuscript.

WAR DIARY
or
INTELLIGENCE SUMMARY
(Erase heading not required.)

Army Form C. 2118

Place	Date	Hour	Summary of Events and Information	Remarks and references to Appendices
Trenches Flamengrie sector	1/8/17 to 2/8/17	6 pm to 6 am	A patrol of two NCOs & four men examined Listening Post in front of enemies lines which was found to be vacant. A very quiet period throughout.	
	2/8/17 to	6 am to 6 pm	rain fell most of the day, & Artillery was quiet on both sides in consequence	
	3/8/17	6 pm to 10 am	rain continued & night was quiet & following day was very quiet.	
	to 3/8/17	6 am to 8 pm	The Battalion was relieved by the 2/5th South Lancs Reg at 8 pm & returned to Billets in Brigade Reserve round ERQUINGHEM except B Company which remained in subsidiary line at MOAT FARM	
	4/8/17		Lieut Colonel E.V. MANGER assumed command of the Battalion.	
	7/8/17		A Company relieved B Company at MOAT FARM and B Company returned to rest Billets	
	11/8/17	6 pm	The Battalion relieved the 2/5th South Lancs Reg at 8 pm relief completed at 10 pm	
	12/8/17	6 am	A quiet night along our front	
		6 am to 6 pm	Our Artillery carried out heavy Bombardment on enemy's Back areas & TMB fired from our right subsector on enemy wire. retaliation light.	
		6 pm	Artillery again active on enemy Back areas.	
	13/8/17	1 am	A Patrol proceeded towards enemy lines composed 1 NCO & 9 men opposite our right subsector to examine enemy wire after TMB shoot. They encountered large enemy working party with covering party. Patrol withdrew & our Artillery was immediately put on to the enemy.	EVManger Lt Col

L.J. Thin
Major

1875 Wt. W593/826 1,000,000 4/15 J.B.C. & A. A.D.S.S./Forms/C. 2118.

Instructions regarding War Diaries and Intelligence Summaries are contained in F. S. Regs., Part II. and the Staff Manual respectively. Title Pages will be prepared in manuscript.

WAR DIARY
or
INTELLIGENCE SUMMARY
(Erase heading not required.)

Army Form C. 2118

Place	Date Aug.	Hour	Summary of Events and Information	Remarks and references to Appendices
	12/13	6p-6am	A Special Patrol at 2 am proceeded along the whole of our front line examining gaps between our posts & reported the line all correct. A Patrol of 1 officer & 4 men examined wire on our left subsector which was reported on.	
	13	6am to 6pm	Our Artillery & Medium Trench Mortars were very active in the afternoon enemy retaliated fairly heavily on our front & support line.	
	13	6pm to	Our Artillery kept up their activity until 9 pm	
	14	1 am	A Patrol of 1 NCO & 9 men proceeded to examine wire in front of our centre subsector, & reported TMBs had made two good gaps in enemy wire.	
	14	1 am to 6 pm	quiet day, nothing unusual.	
	14/15	6p-6am	Continual Patrolling during the night.	
	15	6am to 6p	Quiet day nothing unusual.	
	15	6p-6a	Patrols & listening Posts were out in front of the Trenches but no contact with enemy.	
	16	6am/6p	quiet day.	
	16/17	6p/6a	Two Bangalore Torpedoes successfully exploded in enemy wire.	
	17	6a/6p	MTM Fired on enemy trenches, & retaliation was fairly heavy. the enemy putting about 130 shells on to the Sector.	
	17/18	6p/6a	Patrols active all along our front. five different parties operating.	
	18	6am/6p	quiet day	
	18/19	6p/6a	Patrols out as usual.	
	19	6a/6p	At 2.30pm. 700 Gas Projectors put over Enemy's Line. In evening this Batt. was relieved by 2/5 S. Lancs Regt. Erquinghem Rest Billets occupied	Appx. 11 Col

S. J. Thin
Major

1875 Wt. W593/826 1,000,000 4/15 J.B.C. & A. A.D.S.S./Forms/C. 2118.

Instructions regarding War Diaries and Intelligence Summaries are contained in F. S. Regs., Part II. and the Staff Manual respectively. Title Pages will be prepared in manuscript.

WAR DIARY
or
INTELLIGENCE SUMMARY
(Erase heading not required.)

Army Form C. 2118

Place	Date Aug	Hour	Summary of Events and Information	Remarks and references to Appendices
	20th		Inspection by CO of all Lewis Guns in the Battn. Coy training. Baths	
	21st		Inspection of B. Coy by CO. Coy training	
	22nd		Training all day in Rest Billets all day. Specialists under Specialist Officers	
	23rd		D Coy was relieved by C Coy (took over duties of 5th Coy in Subsidiary Line). D Coy to Rest Billets [at Streaky Bacon Coy training & Baths	
	24th		Inspection of all Specialists at Hqrs by CO. Coy training. A Coy held in readiness to move at once [if necessary by day B Coy by night Medical Inspection of A. B & D Coys.	
	25th		Divine Service at Rolanderie Farm (C of E) Non-Conformists Erquinghem. RCs Erquinghem Church	
	26th		Baths for 3 Coys. A. B. D.	
	27th		This Battn relieved 2/5th S. Lancs Regt in Flamengrie Sub-Sector Relief complete 10.35 pm	
	28th	6 am to 6 pm	Very quiet all day. Heavy Rain. Our MTMs fired from Safety Alley on Indian Trench. Enemy retaliated with Pineapples & a few whizzbangs.	
	28/29th	6 pm to 6 am	Organized programme of fire by night including Artillery. MGs. LGs & Rapid Rifle fire. Extremely little retaliation from enemy	
	29th	6 am to 6 pm	Slight shelling by 18 pdrs on Income Trench & back areas by the Heavies. Stokes T.M. fired on [illegible] Trench. Extremely slight retaliation by enemy principally Pineapples	
	29/30th	6 pm to 6 am	Organized programme of fire by Artillery, MGs, LGs & Rapid Rifle Fire. 3 Patrols left our trenches at 1 am, successfully laid listening sets in No Man's Land, 1 set each side of Bridoux Salient & 1 to the left of Stanway Avenue	

G B L Rae Capt.

1875 Wt. W593/826 1,000,000 4/15 J.B.C. & A. A.D.S.S./Forms/C. 2118.

Instructions regarding War Diaries and Intelligence Summaries are contained in F. S. Regs., Part II. and the Staff Manual respectively. Title Pages will be prepared in manuscript.

WAR DIARY
or
INTELLIGENCE SUMMARY
(Erase heading not required.)

Army Form C. 2118

Place	Date Aug	Hour	Summary of Events and Information	Remarks and references to Appendices
	30th	6 am to 6 pm	Artillery fired in retaliation to enemy's T.M. fire - enemy artillery more active. Jocks' Fry Rue & College Green being shelled with whizzbangs. Several minnies on [illegible] of Safety alley	
	30/31st	6 pm to 6 am	Organized fire by Artillery, Stokes, MGs, LGs & Rifle fire on trenches, incomplete & support trenches. Slight retaliation by Pineapples	
	31st	6 am to 6 pm	Combined artillery & T.M. shoot on enemy's front system. Retaliation negligible.	E.M. Lt Col

1875 Wt. W593/826 1.000.000 4/15 J.B.C. & A. A.D.S.S./Forms/C. 2118.

Confidential

8 G

Vol 8

War Diary.

of.

The 2/9th Battalion "The King's" (Liverpool) Regt.

From. 1st September 1917 To 30th September 1917.

(Volume. VIII.)

WAR DIARY
or
INTELLIGENCE SUMMARY
(Erase heading not required.)

Army Form C. 2118

Instructions regarding War Diaries and Intelligence Summaries are contained in F. S. Regs., Part II. and the Staff Manual respectively. Title Pages will be prepared in manuscript.

Place	Date	Hour	Summary of Events and Information	Remarks and references to Appendices
Trenches FLAMENGRIE SUB SECTOR	1.9.17	Night 31/8 1/9	Quiet period. Bright Moon at night. Three patrols went out to obtain identification. All were heavily fired on when half way across No Mans land. One casualty (wounded) three others had M.G. bullets through clothing. patrols withdrew.	[illegible]
	2.9.17		Quiet period. No Patrolling during night owing to bright Moon.	
			Special Enterprise 2nd Lt L. J. LOCON and Corpl J PRINGLE left our front line breastwork at 10 am and crossed NO MANS LAND in green crawling suits to reconnoitre the Enemy's support line, and the condition of the ground and wire in front of same, opposite our left sub sector. They found the Enemy front line unoccupied, but concrete dugouts in good repair. The parados in front line much damaged. They looked over Enemy front line breastwork and obtained an excellent view of his support line and Switch line. The wire in front of the support line was thick, consisting of Iron Knife rests. The support line appeared in good condition + lower in level than the front line. The Communication trenches from front to support line were very low + in bad repair. Patrol returned without being discovered. Before leaving Enemy front line this officer + N.C.O placed two black aiming boards on Enemy front line breastwork.	[illegible]

1875 Wt. W593/826 1,000,000 4/15 J.B.C. & A. A.D.S.S./Forms/C. 2118.

Instructions regarding War Diaries and Intelligence Summaries are contained in F. S. Regs., Part II. and the Staff Manual respectively. Title Pages will be prepared in manuscript.

WAR DIARY
or
INTELLIGENCE SUMMARY
(Erase heading not required.)

Army Form C. 2118

Place	Date	Hour	Summary of Events and Information	Remarks and references to Appendices
Trenches FLAMENGRIE SUBSECTOR	3.9.17		Night of 2/3 no patrol owing to bright moonlight Quiet day. At 8.55 pm in order to ascertain if the Enemy held his front line in strength, and what portion if any was unoccupied a flare composed of old explosive was fired close to the Enemy wire. This gave us the required information. The enemy appeared to take the flare & smoke for a gas attack. Many Very lights were fired & whistles & horns blown. Our artillery opened on his front & support lines where held thickest.	[illegible]
	4.9.17		Enemy artillery active behind our front line system. At about 5 pm the enemy retaliated to our Medium TM shoot one heavy Minnenwerfer fell on the breastwork of our extreme right post garrisoned by [illegible] B Coy. killing four men and burying five others who were all wounded. The entombed men were quickly dug out by the survivors under the supervision of the Medical Officer and Chaplain. The Battalion was relieved at 8 pm by the 2/5 South Lancs. Regt less A in Subsidiary line - the battalion & returned to billets outside ERQUINGHAM in Brigade Reserve.	[illegible]

Instructions regarding War Diaries and Intelligence Summaries are contained in F. S. Regs., Part II. and the Staff Manual respectively. Title Pages will be prepared in manuscript.

WAR DIARY
or
INTELLIGENCE SUMMARY
(Erase heading not required.)

Army Form C. 2118

Place	Date	Hour	Summary of Events and Information	Remarks and references to Appendices
[illegible] FLAMENGRIE SUBSECTOR	3.9.17		Night of 2/3 no patrol owing to bright moonlight Quiet day At 8.55 pm in order to ascertain if the enemy held his front line in strength and what portion of Army was unoccupied a flare composed of old explosive was fired close to the enemy wire. This gave us the required information. The enemy appeared to take the flare & smoke for a gas attack. Many very lights were fired & whistles & horns blown. Our artillery opened on his front & support lines where held thickest.	BM
	4.9.17		Enemy artillery active behind our front line system. At about 5 pm the enemy retaliated to our Medium TM shoot. One heavy Minnenwerfer fell on the breastwork of our extreme right post garrisoned by 6th B Coy, killing four men and burying five others who were all wounded. The entombed men were quickly dug out by the survivors under the supervision of the Medical Officer and Chaplain. The Battalion was relieved at [illegible] pm by the 2/5 South Lancs R[illegible] & in [illegible] ERQUINGHAM [illegible] in Subsidiary line. The battalion relieved [illegible] in Brigade Reserve	BM

1875 Wt. W593/826 1,000,000 4/15 J.B.C. & A. A.D.S.S./Forms/C. 2118.

Army Form C. 2118

Instructions regarding War Diaries and Intelligence Summaries are contained in F. S. Regs., Part II. and the Staff Manual respectively. Title Pages will be prepared in manuscript.

WAR DIARY
or
INTELLIGENCE SUMMARY
(Erase heading not required.)

Place	Date	Hour	Summary of Events and Information	Remarks and references to Appendices
In Brigade Reserve: BOIS GRENIER Sectr near ERQUINGHEM	5.9.17		Inspections and baths	OHM
	6.9.17		Routine. 64 O.R. sent to be trained under Brigade Lewis gun officer. At night one Company wiring in front line system. One Company finding Brigade duties	OHM
	7.9.17		Inspections, routine. One Company wiring as on 6th inst. One Company finding Brigade duties.	OHM
	8.9.17		Training under Company Commanders. A Co was relieved in the Subsidiary line by B Co.	OHM
	9.9.17		Parade Service. At night one Company wiring in front line system. One Coy finding Brigade duties	OHM
	10.9.17		Training & routine. One Company wiring in front line system	OHM
	11.9.17		Inspection of Kits and clothing.	OHM
	12.9.17		The Battalion relieved the 2/5 SOUTH LANCS Regt at 7.30pm relief complete 9.25pm	OHM

1875 Wt. W593/826 1,000,000 4/15 J.B.C. & A. A.D.S.S./Forms/C. 2118.

Instructions regarding War Diaries and Intelligence Summaries are contained in F. S. Regs., Part II. and the Staff Manual respectively. Title Pages will be prepared in manuscript.

WAR DIARY
or
INTELLIGENCE SUMMARY
(Erase heading not required.)

Army Form C. 2118

Place	Date	Hour	Summary of Events and Information	Remarks and references to Appendices
FLAMENGRIE SUBSECTOR BOIS GRENIER SECTOR	13/9/17		Very quiet period. Repair and improvement of trenches	E.J.M.
	14/9/17		Period of inactivity Trenches thoroughly salved	E.J.M.
	15/9/17		Quiet, Enemy inactive. Wiring done in front of posts	E.J.M.
	16/9/17		Very quiet period Parties of 14th Bn Royal Welsh Fusiliers arrived to see line previous to taking over the Sub Sector.	E.J.M.
	17/9/17		Quiet period This Battalion was relieved by the 14th Bn Royal Welsh Fusiliers relief commenced at 7.30pm & was completed at 9.25pm This Bn to billets in the village of Sailly for the nights of the 17th & 18th	E.J.M.

1875 Wt. W593/826 1,000,000 4/15 J.B.C. & A. A.D.S.S./Forms/C. 2118.

Army Form C. 2118

Instructions regarding War Diaries and Intelligence Summaries are contained in F. S. Regs., Part II. and the Staff Manual respectively. Title Pages will be prepared in manuscript.

WAR DIARY
or
INTELLIGENCE SUMMARY
(Erase heading not required.)

Place	Date	Hour	Summary of Events and Information	Remarks and references to Appendices
Village of SAILLY	18/9/17		Bn remained in SAILLY village and had baths and a complete change of clothing	EHM
	19/9/17	8am	Bn marched to Brigade rendezvous at LAGORGUE, passing the starting point at 9.35 am. & marched via ESTAIRES. LAGORGUE LESTREM to the cross roads HINGES where the Bn broke off & marched independently to billets in the village of Mt. BERNENCHON, where they billeted for the night. An hours halt was made at noon for dinner. The men though somewhat soft marched well & none fell out. Total marched about 14 miles. Time occupied including halts 7½ hours. The band & the mid-day halt were invaluable in preventing fatigue. Men bathed their feet on arrival at Mt BERNENCHON	EHM

1875 Wt. W593/826 1,000,000 4/15 J.B.C. & A. A.D.S.S./Forms/C. 2118.

Instructions regarding War Diaries and Intelligence Summaries are contained in F. S. Regs., Part II. and the Staff Manual respectively. Title Pages will be prepared in manuscript.

WAR DIARY
or
INTELLIGENCE SUMMARY
(Erase heading not required.)

Army Form C. 2118

Place	Date	Hour	Summary of Events and Information	Remarks and references to Appendices
	20/9/17	8 am	The Battn left MT. BERNENCHON at 8 am and proceeded to Bgde Starting Point at the Cross Roads in BAS RIEUX passing starting point at 10.38 am. Route BAS RIEUX – LILLERS – BOURECQ – south of St HILAIRE – WESTERHEM to the cross roads 400 yds south of A in FEBVIN-PALFART thence by Companies to Billets in FEBVIN-PALFART and HONENGHEM: there were the usual halts including 1 hour for dinners. The Battn arrived in Billets by 3.30 pm no men fell out – marching good.	[illegible]
	21/9/17		Day devoted to cleaning of equipment & interior economy	[illegible]
	22/9/17		Inspection of all Companies & Specialists by C.O. Coys at disposal of Coy Commanders	[illegible]
	23/9/17		Parade Service in Battn Parade Ground at 11.30 am. RC's at FEBVIN-PALFART 9 am.	[illegible]
	24/9/17		Training commenced according to Bgde Programme – including Ceremonial March Past. In the afternoon Kit Inspection of the whole Battn.	[illegible]
	25/9/17		Training in morning & Games in afternoon – 1 Coy on the Range.	
	26/9/17		Training in morning & Games in afternoon – 1 Coy on the Range.	[illegible]
	27/9/17		Training & Baths in morning – 1 Coy on Range. Inspection by GOC 57th Divn at 2.30 pm followed by March Past including Transport. Lecture by Major Anderson 1st Army Instructor in PT & BF at 3.15 pm. Games in the evening.	
	28/9/17		Training according to Programme in morning. Games in the afternoon. 1 Coy on the Range. 2 Coys fitted with new containers for Box Respirators.	

1875 Wt. W593/826 1,000,000 4/15 J.B.C. & A. A.D.S.S./Forms/C. 2118.

Instructions regarding War Diaries and Intelligence Summaries are contained in F. S. Regs., Part II. and the Staff Manual respectively. Title Pages will be prepared in manuscript.

WAR DIARY
or
INTELLIGENCE SUMMARY
(Erase heading not required.)

Army Form C. 2118

Place	Date	Hour	Summary of Events and Information	Remarks and references to Appendices
HONENGHEM	29/9/17	8 am	Routine & Training in the morning – 1 Coy at the Range. Games in the afternoon.	OHM
	30/9/17	"	Divine Service C of E on Battn Parade Ground 10.30 am. RCs gen at FEBVIN-PALFART. Nonconformists 11 am at FLECHIN.	OHM
			AWARDS	
	30/9/17	"	No 332025 Cpl. James BARRETT was this day awarded a Divisional Gallantry Card by G.O.C. 57th Division for gallant conduct & devotion to duty in the Field on 4. Sept. 1917 in the front line Trenches at BOIS-GRENIER Sector near ARMENTIERES.	OHM
			No 332162 Pte SAMUEL WILLIAMS was on the same date awarded a Divisional Gallantry Card for gallant conduct & devotion to duty on the same date	

O. V. Hi[illegible] Lt Col

Commdg 2/9 Bn. The Kings (Liverpool Regt)

1875 Wt. W593/826 1,000,000 4/15 J.B.C. & A. A.D.S.S./Forms/C. 2118.

Confidential

98

War Diary

of.

4119

2/9th Battalion "The King's" (Liverpool) Regt.

From 1st October 1917. To. 31st October 1917

Volume.......

Instructions regarding War Diaries and Intelligence Summaries are contained in F. S. Regs., Part II. and the Staff Manual respectively. Title pages will be prepared in manuscript.

WAR DIARY
or
INTELLIGENCE SUMMARY.
(Erase heading not required.)

Army Form C. 2118.

Hour, Date, Place	Summary of Events and Information	Remarks and references to Appendices
HONENGHEM 1st Oct 1917 EHM	General routine Battalion Training	EHM
2nd Oct, "	do Night operations, of little value owing to bright moonlight.	EHM
3rd Oct. "	General routine Battalion Training	EHM
4th Oct, "	General routine, Men bathed. Officers instructed in the reading of Aeroplane photographs. More instruction would be valuable. Few officers are able to read these photographs	EHM
5th Oct "	General routine. Night Operation (Assembly for attack)	EHM

(73989) W4141—463. 400,000. 9/14. H.&J.Ltd. Forms/C. 2118/10.

Instructions regarding War Diaries and Intelligence Summaries are contained in F. S. Regs., Part II. and the Staff Manual respectively. Title pages will be prepared in manuscript.

WAR DIARY
or
INTELLIGENCE SUMMARY.
(Erase heading not required.)

Army Form C. 2118.

Hour, Date, Place	Summary of Events and Information	Remarks and references to Appendices
HONENGHEM 6th Oct 1917	Inspection of the 172 Infantry Brigade by Field Marshal Sir Douglas Haig.	ODM
7th Oct "	The Battalion attended Divine Service.	ODM
8th Oct "	Battalion Training and General routine	ODM
9th Oct "	General routine. Brigade night operation. Battalion marched out at 12 mn	ODM
10th Oct "	Battalion returned to billets at 11.30 am.	ODM
11th Oct "	General routine. Battalion Trench to Trench attack. Afternoon Baths & Brigade Sports, at which the regiment won the tug of war, and Signalling Competitions. The latter combining training with sport was most keenly taken up by the men.	ODM

(73989) W4141—463. 400,000. 9/14. H.&J.Ltd. Forms/C. 2118/10.

Instructions regarding War Diaries and Intelligence Summaries are contained in F.S. Regs., Part II. and the Staff Manual respectively. Title pages will be prepared in manuscript.

WAR DIARY
or
INTELLIGENCE SUMMARY.
(Erase heading not required.)

Army Form C. 2118.

Hour, Date, Place	Summary of Events and Information	Remarks and references to Appendices
HONENGHEM 12th Oct, 1917	General routine. Bn Training	EDM
13th Oct. "	Brigade Trench to Trench attack in heavy rain.	EDM
14th Oct. "	Bright & cold. Voluntary Services	EDM
15th Oct,	General routine. Clipping of all transport animals & officers chargers except mules.	EDM
	Battalion training in forenoon. Transport Sports afternoon.	EDM
16th Oct.	Training & baths. Average daily sick from 1st to 16th Oct ten. The rations have been excellent, & the regimental Cooks take great interest in the preparation of the food which is varied and appetising.	

Instructions regarding War Diaries and Intelligence Summaries are contained in F. S. Regs., Part II. and the Staff Manual respectively. Title pages will be prepared in manuscript.

WAR DIARY
or
INTELLIGENCE SUMMARY.
(Erase heading not required.)

Army Form C. 2118.

Hour, Date, Place	Summary of Events and Information	Remarks and references to Appendices
HONENGHEM 17. Oct. 1917	The G.O.C. Brigade inspected the Battn carrying out Trench to Trench attack	E.M.
18 Oct	This Unit marched with the Brigade to Billets in RENESCURE (AREA)	E.M.
19 Oct	The Battn embussed with the Brigade & arrived in PROVEN area. Transport moved by road	E.M.
PROVEN AREA 20 Oct	The day was devoted to a general inspection of all Kit etc	E.M.
Refce HAZEBROUCK 5a 1/100000 area H.2. 21 Oct	Battn Church Parade at 10 am. RCs at PROVEN church 10.20 am Presbyterians Non-Conformists 11 am at 2/10th K.R.R. Camp	E.M.
22 Oct	In the morning the Assembly Formation was practised also at 7.30 pm On leaving 1st Army all indents for the last 14 days were cancelled – this is a dangerous practice & may result in a Unit arriving in a Battle area ill-provided – especially so in Boots & Leather. This system would appear very easy of amendment.	E.M.
23 Oct	C. Coy reported to aerodrome for working party – the other Companies at the disposal of Coy Commanders	E.M.
24. Oct	The morning was spent in packing up & the paying of 3 Companies – B. Coy reported to aerodrome for working party. In the afternoon the Battn marched to PITCHCOTT Camp	E.M.
25. Oct	B. Coy was payed. A Coy reported to Aerodrome for working party. The 3 remaining Coys at disposal of Coy Commanders. The Sentence by F.G.C.M. on Pte Wainwright was promulgated on Battn Parade. Overstaying leave 4 days, award 91 days F.P. No 1.	E.M.

(73989) W4141–463. 400,000. 9/14. H.&J.Ltd. Forms/C. 2118/10.

Instructions regarding War Diaries and Intelligence Summaries are contained in F. S. Regs., Part II. and the Staff Manual respectively. Title pages will be prepared in manuscript.

WAR DIARY
or
INTELLIGENCE SUMMARY.
(Erase heading not required.)

Army Form C. 2118.

Hour, Date, Place	Summary of Events and Information	Remarks and references to Appendices
26. Oct. 1917 PROVEN AREA	Final Inspection by Coy Commanders before moving into Battle Area. 10.30pm received orders to entrain at 12 midnight at PROVEN. Heavy rain during day making it difficult to leave Transport lines. Train arrived ELVERDINGHE about 1.45 am - held up owing to Bombs.	EKM
27 Oct. 1917 MALAKOFF AREA Refce Sheet Belgium 28 NW Edition 6a $\frac{1}{20,000}$ (B22b)	Arrived SOULT CAMP in MALAKOFF area about 4 am. - Camp exceedingly muddy & difficult to place men in as details of [illegible] still in Camp. Transport by Road arrived 7 am	EKM
28 Oct. 1917	Inspection by CO of Companies in Battle order. Firing Party of 12 under Lieut LEE JONES found for funeral of RFA officers. 2nd in C. OC Companies & Specialist Officers reconnoitred Battle Area during day. Drying Tent erected.	" EKM
29. Oct. 1917	The Battn practised formations to be used in advancing to re-inforce or counter attack from support positions - the men being distributed in sections in shell holes etc previous to the advance. Reconnaissance of Battle area by remaining officers & Runners.	EKM
30. Oct. 1917	Inspection & re-fitting of Battn for the Line. Heavy enemy bombing of Camp area at night. Further Reconnaissance by Officers & Runners of the Line	EKM
31. Oct. 1917	Coy under Coy arrangements - Inspection in the afternoon of all Coys in Battle order. Reconnaissance by Officers, Scouts & Runners of COMPROMIS FARM area (Refce SCHAAP BALIE $\frac{1}{10000}$). Orders received to take over Front Line system & Posts on night of 2/3rd Nov. Heavy enemy Bombing at night.	EKM

E.K. Munger Lt Col.
Commdg [illegible]

Vol 10

Confidential.

10g

War Diary

of

2/9th Battalion "The King's" (Liverpool) Regiment.

From 1st November 1917 To. 30th November 1917.

Volume

Army Form C. 2118.

Instructions regarding War Diaries and Intelligence Summaries are contained in F. S. Regs., Part II. and the Staff Manual respectively. Title pages will be prepared in manuscript.

WAR DIARY
or
INTELLIGENCE SUMMARY.
(Erase heading not required.)

Hour, Date, Place	Summary of Events and Information	Remarks and references to Appendices
MALAKOFF AREA 1. Nov. 1917.	Inspection of Coys. in Battle order by C.O. Heavy enemy bombing at night.	GBLR
SCHAAP BALIE 2. Nov. 1917	Left SOULT CAMP 9.30 am arrived MARSOUIN CAMP 11 am. where hot dinners were given to the Battn. Each man had his feet rubbed in whale oil for previous 7 days and 1 "Tommy Cooker" was supplied to every 3rd man. Each man carried a small oil-can of rum for emergencies. This system proved to be of the greatest benefit as the weather was cold & the ground very damp. At 5 pm proceeded to Front line System & relieved 2/8th KLR; although shelled on the way up remarkably few casualties only 5 wounded. Relief complete 10 pm. MEMLING FARM was handed over by 2/8th KLR & occupied by this Unit; withdrawal from this advanced post was ordered by Brigade the post being untenable & tactically useless: 1 O.R. killed during occupation of post.	GBLR
3 Nov 1917.	5.30 am inspection of Battn. dispositions by G.O.C. 172nd Inf. Brigade, each Platoon had formed a Strong Point; these are to be linked up later to form a Front Line system of Trenches. See attached Map 3.	GBLR GBL Rae Major 2/9th King's Liverpool Regt

(73989) W4141—463. 400,000. 9/14. H.&J.Ltd. Forms/C. 2118/10.

Instructions regarding War Diaries and Intelligence Summaries are contained in F. S. Regs., Part II. and the Staff Manual respectively. Title pages will be prepared in manuscript.

WAR DIARY
or
INTELLIGENCE SUMMARY.
(Erase heading not required.)

Army Form C. 2118.

Hour, Date, Place	Summary of Events and Information	Remarks and references to Appendices
SCHAAP BALIE 3 NOV. 1917.	Orders received at 3.45 pm to send out 3 Patrols – 1 to reconnoitre MEMLING FARM, 1 to reconnoitre some concrete dug-outs approximately at Point V.8 a 1.5 and 1 to reconnoitre as far forward as possible to SPIDER CROSS ROADS. The Patrol found MEMLING FARM occupied by MG & the enemy in neighbouring shell-holes & returned after being fired on. The Patrol ordered to Point V.8 a 1.5 did not proceed as the left advanced post of the Company had during day moved up to this position – the shell holes were sandbagged but not concreted. The Patrol ordered for reconnaissance of SPIDER CROSS ROADS were caught in a heavy enemy barrage & 7 men were affected by Gas – after lying out for over an hour 2Lt [illegible] brought his party back to LOUIS FARM & handed men affected by Gas to M.O. About 11 pm a deserter from the German lines surrendered to a post of A Coy: he was at once sent down to Bde HQrs for examination. Heavy enemy Barrage continued till after midnight. Casualties 1 killed 3 wounded	GBLR G B L Rae Major 2/7th King's [illegible]

(73989) W4141—463. 400,000. 9/14. H.&J.Ltd. Forms/C. 2118/10.

Instructions regarding War Diaries and Intelligence Summaries are contained in F. S. Regs., Part II. and the Staff Manual respectively. Title pages will be prepared in manuscript.

WAR DIARY
or
INTELLIGENCE SUMMARY.
(Erase heading not required.)

Army Form C. 2118.

Hour, Date, Place	Summary of Events and Information	Remarks and references to Appendices
SCHAAP BALIE 4. Nov. 1917	C.O. went round the line in the morning & 2nd in Command in the afternoon. Great enemy aerial activity in the afternoon over the lines: English aeroplanes not in evidence. Battn relief by 2/10th K.L.R. commenced at 5 pm. From 4 pm onwards there was very heavy enemy bombardment between LANGEMARCK CORNER and BONGITE [?] which continued until well after midnight and the Battn suffered considerable casualties including Capt. R.A. Moultfield [?] (Killed) Lieut Col E.V. Manger [?] (wounded) & Capt & Adjt J. Lought [?] (wounded). The Battn brought down a considerable amount of Salvage including 8 Lewis Guns & 42 Rifles (see attached list). Salvage dumped at HUDDLESTONE CAMP. In view of the most trying conditions coming out of the line this was most creditable.	GBLR [?]
HUDDLESTONE CAMP 5 Nov. 1917	Battn arrived HUDDLESTONE CAMP between 1 am & 4 am when all the men were given Hot-tea mixed with rum before turning in. At 4.30 am Camp shelled by H.V. Shells 4 O.R. wounded	GBLR [?]

G.B.L. Rose [illegible] Major
2/9th King's Liverpool Regt.

(73989) W4141–463. 400,000. 9/14. H.&J.Ltd. Forms/C. 2118/10.

Instructions regarding War Diaries and Intelligence Summaries are contained in F. S. Regs., Part II. and the Staff Manual respectively. Title pages will be prepared in manuscript.

WAR DIARY
or
INTELLIGENCE SUMMARY.
(Erase heading not required.)

Army Form C. 2118.

Hour, Date, Place	Summary of Events and Information	Remarks and references to Appendices
HUDDLESTONE CAMP 5 Nov 1917	Major G.B.L. Rae assumed temporary command of the Batt. & Lieut F.B. Clement took over the duties of Adjutant. Capt R.A. Mountfield was buried at SOULT CAMP Cemetery at 3pm. the service was taken by the Revd E. Fisher the Regimental Chaplain. At 5pm the Batt. moved to MARSOUIN CAMP to Bivouac Tents.	GBLR
6 Nov 1917	At dawn the Camp was shelled by HE & H.V. Shell which continued until 4.30 pm. Total Casualties for this Tour in the Line: 1 Officer & 13 O.R. killed, and 6 missing. 34 wounded = 54 Casualties. NB. 1 of the missing has been accounted for & was buried by 2/10th KLR Burials by this Batt. of men of other Regts 100. At 8pm the Batt. was relieved by 10th Bn Lancashire Fusiliers and moved to BRIDGE CAMP, ELVERDINGHE The following officer NCO & men did conspicuously good work in the line & their names brought to the notice of G.O.C. 171st Inf. Brigade – Capt Philip McRitchie RAMC(T) attd 2/9th KLR no 331604 Sergt Delmas L.L. no 331863 Pte Barkley I. no 332062 Pte Humphrey E.	GBLR
7 Nov 1917 Rifle Maj. HAZEBROUCK 5A	The Batt. left ELVERDINGHE by train at 12 noon for AUDRUICQ and arrived in Rest Billets at NIELLES about 10.30pm	GBLR GBL Rae Major 2/9th Kings Liverpool R

(73989) W4141—463. 400,000. 9/14. H.&J.Ltd. Forms/C. 2118/10.

Instructions regarding War Diaries and Intelligence Summaries are contained in F. S. Regs., Part II. and the Staff Manual respectively. Title pages will be prepared in manuscript.

WAR DIARY
or
INTELLIGENCE SUMMARY.
(Erase heading not required.)

Army Form C. 2118.

Hour, Date, Place	Summary of Events and Information	Remarks and references to Appendices
NIELLES 8. Nov. 1917	Kit inspection by O.C. Companies in the afternoon. All Ranks rested in the morning	SBLR
9. Nov. 1917	The Battn paraded at 9 am under Coy Commanders and all Kit deficiencies were taken. At 11 am the C.O. inspected the Battn. Parade dismissed at 12.30 pm. All H.Q.rs personnel bathed also Transport.	SBLR
10. Nov. 1917	Parade cancelled owing to bad weather. A Coy bathed. The draft of 5 officers & 37 O.R.s were inspected by C.O. in the afternoon	SBLR
11. Nov. 1917	Church Parades cancelled owing to bad weather. Holy Communion held at B.H.Q. at 12 noon	SBLR
12 Nov 1917	Training carried out in accordance with Bde Programme. Lewis Gun teams inspected by Brigade Lewis Gun Officer. Captain E.A. Wilkinson took over duties as Second-in-Command. Lieut J.M. Parker took over command of D Coy. One Company bathed during afternoon	SEAW

Edward Wilkinson Capt.
[illegible] Regt.

Instructions regarding War Diaries and Intelligence Summaries are contained in F. S. Regs., Part II. and the Staff Manual respectively. Title pages will be prepared in manuscript.

WAR DIARY
or
INTELLIGENCE SUMMARY.
(Erase heading not required.)

Army Form C. 2118.

Hour, Date, Place	Summary of Events and Information	Remarks and references to Appendices
NIELLES Nov 13th 1917	Training in accordance with Bde Programme	[illegible]
14th "	Training in accordance with Bde Programme. Special class for Lewis Gunners started lasting three days. Letter received from G.O.C. & Officers of 170th Infty Bde thanking Lt Col E.V. Manger and officers of 2/9th Bn "The Kings" for sending their Band to PROVEN to cheer up the men of the 170th Infty Bde who had come out of the line. Coys Sports held on Company Training Area	[illegible]
15th	Coys trained in accordance with Bde Programme. Lecture in the afternoon by A.D.M.S. 57th Division on "Trench Foot" for which the battalion paraded	[illegible]
16th	Training in accordance with Bde Programme. Special attention paid to Saluting. Two Coys bathed	[illegible]
17th	Battalion paraded at 8.30 am and marched to GUEMY Rifle Range for firing practice	[illegible]
18th	Church Parade on Battalion parade ground at 11.30 am	[illegible]

[illegible] Wilkinson Capt
[illegible]

Instructions regarding War Diaries and Intelligence Summaries are contained in F. S. Regs., Part II. and the Staff Manual respectively. Title pages will be prepared in manuscript.

WAR DIARY
or
INTELLIGENCE SUMMARY.
(Erase heading not required.)

Army Form C. 2118.

Hour, Date, Place	Summary of Events and Information	Remarks and references to Appendices
NIELLES		
Nov 19th 1917	Training in accordance with Brigade Programme	[initials]
" 20th "	Training in accordance with Brigade Programme	[initials]
" 21st "	Training in accordance with Brigade Programme	[initials]
" 22nd "	Battalion paraded and marched to the Fifth Army Musketry Range for firing practice.	[initials]
" 23rd "	Inspection of Battalion by G.O.C. 51st Division	[initials]
	Lt Col E.V. Manger returned to unit from hospital	
	Band of the 73rd French Infantry Regiment visited the Battalion and played on the parade ground	
" 24th "	Battalion practice attack carried out on RECQUES WEST Training area.	[initials]
" 25th "	Parade Service 11.30 am	[initials]
" 26th "	Training in accordance with Brigade Programme	[initials]
" 27th "	Training in accordance with Brigade Programme	[initials]
" 28th "	Battalion Attack practice. RECQUES WEST area	[initials]

[signature] Capt. [illegible]

(73989) W4141–463. 400,000. 9/14. H.&J.Ltd. Forms/C. 2118/10.

Instructions regarding War Diaries and Intelligence Summaries are contained in F. S. Regs., Part II. and the Staff Manual respectively. Title pages will be prepared in manuscript.

WAR DIARY
or
INTELLIGENCE SUMMARY.
(*Erase heading not required.*)

Army Form C. 2118.

Hour, Date, Place	Summary of Events and Information	Remarks and references to Appendices
NIELLES Nov 29th 1917	Training in accordance with Brigade Programme The Corps Commander XIX Corps has awarded the MILITARY MEDAL to the undermentioned for gallantry and devotion to duty in action No 330037 Sergt Johnson J 332062 Pte Hawksley E 331863 Pte Barkley J	[illegible]
Nov 30th 1917	Training in accordance with Brigade Programme	[illegible]

[illegible] Capt
9th Bn [illegible] Regt

(73989) W4141—463. 400,000. 9/14. H.&J.Ltd. Forms/C. 2118/10.

LIST OF SALVAGE BROUGHT OUT OF THE LINE BY 2/9th BATTN."THE KINGS" (LIVERPOOL REGT),& DUMPED AT HUDDLESTON CAMP:--

---

(ON NIGHT OF 4th/5th NOVR,1917).

Lewis Guns.	8.- 4 returned to O.C., 2/8th K.L.R.
Magazines.	9.
Rifles.	39 (3 German) 42.
Bayonets.	13.
Very Pistols.	1.
Wire Cutters, pairs,	3.
Spare Part Bags.	6.
Entrenching Tool Carriers.	13.
Water Bottles.	9.
" Carriers.	14.
Haversacks.	18.
Pouches.	18.
Straps, shoulder.	15.
Belts.	5.
Gas Helmets.	4.
Entrench: Tool Heads.	4.
" " Helves.	8.
Steel Helmets.	1.
Oil Sheets.	2.
Bombs, Bags.	5.
Periscopes.	1.
" Cover.	1.
Petrol Tins.	2.
Telephone, D.III.	1.

Map Reference C.7.d.30.45 - 1/10,000.

Confidential

11.8

Vol. 11

War Diary

of

2/9th Battalion "The King's" (Liverpool) Regt.

Period.

1st December 1917 to 31st December 1917.

Volume ------

Instructions regarding War Diaries and Intelligence Summaries are contained in F. S. Regs., Part II. and the Staff Manual respectively. Title pages will be prepared in manuscript.

WAR DIARY
or
INTELLIGENCE SUMMARY.
(*Erase heading not required.*)

Army Form C. 2118.

Hour, Date, Place	Summary of Events and Information	Remarks and references to Appendices
NIELLES 1. Dec. 1917.	Battn marched to RECQUES WEST area & carried out an attack Practice	GBHR
2 Dec 1917.	Battn Church Parade	GBHR
3 Dec 1917	Training in accordance with Brigade Programme a second Lewis Gun Class started	GBHR
4. Dec. 1917.	Training in accordance with Brigade Programme	GBHR
5. Dec 1917	The Battn took part in a Brigade attack Practice RECQUES.W.	GBHR
6. Dec. 1917.	Demonstration for officers & NCOs by Commandant XVIII Corps School at NORDAUSQUES. Coys at disposal of Coy 2nd in Command	GBHR
	HONOURS & AWARDS	
	The F.M.C. in C awarded the following decorations for gallantry & devotion to duty. The Military Cross Capt. P. McRitchie RAMC attd 2/9th The Kings	
	Bar to Military Medal 331604 Sergt. Delmes L. L 2/9th The King's	
7. Dec. 1917.	The Battn entrained at AUDRUICQ Station & arrived PROVEN 1.30pm from where it march to HERZEELE Rest area	GBHR

GBH Rae Major
Commdg 2/9th King's Liverpool Regt.

(73989) W4141—463. 400,000. 9/14. H.&J.Ltd. Forms/C. 2118/10.

Instructions regarding War Diaries and Intelligence Summaries are contained in F. S. Regs., Part II. and the Staff Manual respectively. Title pages will be prepared in manuscript.

WAR DIARY
or
INTELLIGENCE SUMMARY.
(Erase heading not required.)

Army Form C. 2118.

Hour, Date, Place	Summary of Events and Information	Remarks and references to Appendices
HERZEELE		
8. Dec. 1917	Kit Inspection of the whole Battn. Improving of Billets etc	OHM
9. Dec. 1917	Battn Church Parade 11.30 am. A & B Coys batted	OHM
10. Dec. 1917	Training carried out in accordance with Battn Programme C. Coy bathed.	OHM
11 Dec 1917	Training carried out in accordance with Battn Programme. D. Coy bathed. Battn Inter-Platoon Singing Competition.	OHM
12 Dec. 1917	Inspection of battalion by G.O.C. 172nd Infantry Bde	OHM
13 Dec. 1917	Training in accordance with Battn Programme.	OHM
14 Dec 1917	Training in accordance with Battn. Programme.	OHM
15 Dec 1917	A, B, C Coys Training in accordance with Bn Programme D Coy carried out an attack practice	OHM
16 Dec 1917	Church Parade held in the CINEMA HERZEELE at 10 am. Advance party under Capt. G.H. Wilkinson	OHM

(73989) W4141—463. 400,000. 9/14. H.&J.Ltd. Forms/C. 2118/10.

Instructions regarding War Diaries and Intelligence Summaries are contained in F. S. Regs., Part II. and the Staff Manual respectively. Title pages will be prepared in manuscript.

WAR DIARY
or
INTELLIGENCE SUMMARY.
(Erase heading not required.)

Army Form C. 2118.

Hour, Date, Place	Summary of Events and Information	Remarks and references to Appendices
HERZEELE 16 Dec 1917	proceeded to EMILE CAMP ELVERDINGHE to arrange accomodation for the battalion	[illegible]
EMILE CAMP ELVERDINGHE 17 Dec 1917	The battalion entrained at HERZEELE at 9am and arrived ELVERDINGHE at 12.30 pm. It then proceeded byroad to the Support Brigade area and was accommodated at EMILE CAMP in huts & dugouts. The facilities attained in this camp were very good. The huts were in good condition and fitted with Stoves. Good cookhouses for each company enabled a very good menu to be adhered to each day. Soup tea or porridge was given to the men each night. <u>Transport</u> The Transport was accommodated at BENSONS FARM. The lines and accomodation were Satisfactory. The standings although affording good accommodation were not complete when taken over. They are being improved each day.	[illegible]
		[illegible]

(73989) W4141—463. 400,000. 9/14. H.&J.Ltd. Forms/C. 2118/10.

Instructions regarding War Diaries and Intelligence Summaries are contained in F. S. Regs., Part II. and the Staff Manual respectively. Title pages will be prepared in manuscript.

WAR DIARY
or
INTELLIGENCE SUMMARY.
(Erase heading not required.)

Army Form C. 2118.

Hour, Date, Place	Summary of Events and Information	Remarks and references to Appendices
EMILE CAMP ELVERDINGHE		
18th Dec 1917	Company Commanders reconnoitred Forward Area. Companies paraded under Company arrangements for Cleaning & Kit Inspections.	[illegible]
19th Dec 1917	Training in accordance with Bn Programme. Captain & Adjutant [illegible] Knight mentioned ~~for~~ [illegible] in despatches dated 18 12 17.	[illegible]
20th Dec 1917.	Routine.	[illegible]
21st Dec 1917.	Officers reconnoitred line	[illegible]
22nd Dec 1917.	Training & Routine. Officers reconnoitred Frontline System with NCOs. HOUTHULST Forest Sector.	[illegible]
23 Dec 1917	Divine Service.	[illegible]
24 Dec 1917	Fitting out for going into Line.	[illegible]

WAR DIARY
or
INTELLIGENCE SUMMARY
(Erase heading not required.)

Instructions regarding War Diaries and Intelligence Summaries are contained in F. S. Regs., Part II. and the Staff Manual respectively. Title Pages will be prepared in manuscript.

Army Form C. 2118

Place	Date	Hour	Summary of Events and Information	Remarks and references to Appendices
HOUTHULST FOREST	25	3 pm	The Batt crossed the Canal at 3-15 pm via CLARGES STREET to take over the Left Sub-Sector from the 2/7th Kings Liverpool Regt. Administrative & Operation Order attached. Relief complete 7.45 pm. One Casualty Machine Gun Fire. Frequent heavy falls of snow during the relief & throughout the night. All posts in front line inspected. Most posts had neither adequate protection from fire or any shelter from the weather. The wire along the whole front is negligable. Men worked on posts throughout night. No movement	EHM
	26		allowed by day, wire and corrugated shelters brought up by carrying parties after dusk & improvement of posts continued. Heavy Barrage laid to the right of right Sub-Sector caused enemy on our front uneasiness this he showed by continual shelling and Machine Gun fire on tracks and cross roads and extra alertness along our front posts brilliant moonlight & snow made patrolling impossible. Casualties One Officer 2Lt W.A. Reid & 3 OR Killed 14 OR wounded. 2Lt W.A. Reid and Sgt T.B. Womes were hit whilst visiting the Front Line Posts	EHM

1875 Wt. W593/826 1,000,000 4/15 J.B.C. & A. A.D.S.S./Forms/C. 2118.

Instructions regarding War Diaries and Intelligence Summaries are contained in F. S. Regs., Part II. and the Staff Manual respectively. Title Pages will be prepared in manuscript.

WAR DIARY
or
INTELLIGENCE SUMMARY
(Erase heading not required.)

Army Form C. 2118

Place	Date	Hour	Summary of Events and Information	Remarks and references to Appendices
HOUTHULST FOREST	27	5 AM	Weather still severe ground snow covered & frost bound. One case of Trench Foot. – Two large carrying parties found by Reserve Coy carried up from R.E. Dump to front line [illegible] wire stakes and elephant shelters. Men of front line posts improved shelters & put up wire in Forest. Honours and Awards: For Gallant Services on Western Front 2nd Lt. [illegible] Loram Manchester Regt. attached 4th [illegible] the King's [illegible]. Regt. "Mentioned in Despatches" of Nov 7th "London Gazette" of Tuesday Dec 18th 1917.	ODM
"	"	4.30 pm	Inter Coy. Relief Complete "A" & "B" Coys. relieved "C" & "D" Coys. in the Front Line C & D Coys returning to the Counter Attack & Reserve Coy Lines respectively. Trench Foot: The prescribed precautionary measures for the prevention of Trench Foot appear to be having the desired effect under the most adverse circumstances. Ground very bad thaw set in.	ODM

1875 Wt. W593/826 1,000,000 4/15 J.B.C. & A. A.D.S.S./Forms/C. 2118.

Army Form C. 2118

WAR DIARY
or
INTELLIGENCE SUMMARY
(Erase heading not required.)

Instructions regarding War Diaries and Intelligence Summaries are contained in F. S. Regs., Part II. and the Staff Manual respectively. Title Pages will be prepared in manuscript.

Place	Date	Hour	Summary of Events and Information	Remarks and references to Appendices
HOUTHULST FOREST	28		Front area quiet. Several cases of frost bitten feet amongst the troops relieved from the line shell holes, owing to the men being unable to move about or leave their shell holes. Snow covered ground & bright moonlight making the least movement visable to the enemy. Who on his side had his back to the Forest. Special warning order received regarding the unusual quietness of the enemy from Divisional Commander but the hours of darkness passed away without any unusual occurance. Arrangement	EOM
	29		made with the 2/10th K.L.R. to relieve at 10.30 pm instead of usual time about 8 oclock to avoid the usual period of enemy activity. At 5.20 pm S.O.S. signal was seen on our right & passed on by us. Our barrage responding immediately. Relief carried out without casualty. Total casualties during the four days in the line 1 Officer 4 O/R Killed & One officer (2nd Lt F.R. Hill) & 21 O/R Wounded.	EOM

E.V. Manger Lt Col
Commdg 2/9 Kings (Lpool Regt)

1875 Wt. W593/826 1,000,000 4/15 J.B.C. & A. A.D.S.S./Forms/C. 2118.

Instructions regarding War Diaries and Intelligence Summaries are contained in F. S. Regs., Part II. and the Staff Manual respectively. Title Pages will be prepared in manuscript.

WAR DIARY
or
INTELLIGENCE SUMMARY
(Erase heading not required.)

Army Form C. 2118

Place	Date	Hour	Summary of Events and Information	Remarks and references to Appendices
CANAL BANK	30th Decr 1917	1.45 am	Relief complete, battalion on arriving at CANAL BANK was served out with a hot meal and tea.	OPP
	31st		Three companies employed on fatigues in front line	
		5.30 pm	One composite Company relieved a company of the 2/4 South Lancashire Regt, in the right sub Sector. Arrangement made for housing the relieved Coy. on arrival at Canal Bank. Hot tea and rhum to be served out.	OPW
			Weather Conditions:- Slight thaw in morning followed by hard frost, cold severe. Night clear.	
			Enemy Aeroplanes crossed canal, passing over camp	

E.J. Mangin Lt Col
Commdg 2/9 The King's

1875 Wt. W593/826 1,000,000 4/15 J.B.C. & A. A.D.S.S./Forms/C. 2118.

War Diary

RELIEF ORDERS
BY
LIEUT.COL., E.V.MANGER, COMMANDG,
"X" BATTALION.

IN THE FIELD. 26th DECEMBER, 1917.

???????????????????????

RELIEF:- Inter-Company Relief will take place tomorrow at 11.30.p.m.
"A" Company will relieve "C" Company on the LEFT Coy Sector.
"B" Company will relieve "D" Company on the RIGHT Coy Sector.
Os.C., "C" & "D" Coy will furnish Os.C., "A" & "B" Coy with numbers of posts, strength of each post, and position of Lewis Guns by 6.0.p.m. tomorrow.
Lewis Guns will be taken out but ammunition handed over.
Relieving Teams will come up with one full drum.

GUIDES:- Guides from each post in the front line will await the arrival of relieving posts at point V.6.c.8.3. on the FIVE CHEMINS ROAD at 11.15.p.m.
ANTI-AIRCRAFT POSTS will be handed and taken over as ordinary posts.

MOVE:- Posts will move to the front line in Single file with at least 50 yards' interval between posts.

On relief "C" Coy will take over VEE BEND Area, and "D" Coy will move to CRAONNE FARM by posts as relieved, in Single file.

Relief complete will be reported to Battalion Headquarters by wire, using the following Code Words:-

"A" COMPANY	-	"RED"
"B" "	-	"GREEN"
"C" "	-	"YELLOW"
"D" "	-	"BLUE"

?????????????

H B Clement

Capt & A/Adjt.,
"X" Battalion.

[illegible]

[illegible]

[illegible]

Ref. No. [illegible] [illegible]

1.DETAILS REMAIN-ING BEHIND. Details not proceeding into the line will be accommodated as under:-

CAPT. H.H.WILKINSON.
[illegible] [illegible]

ORDERLY ROOM STAFF.
TRANSPORT PERSONNEL.
BAND. WAGON LINES.
QUARTERMASTER'S STAFF.
BATTN.H/QRS BATMEN.

ALL COY DETAILS:- [illegible] CAMP.

CAPT. [illegible] will be responsible for parading the Coy Details at [illegible] a.m. tomorrow, and taking them to the Camp. He will be responsible for this party until proceeding on leave, when CAPT. H.J.[illegible] will take over.

Each man will take with him the unexpended portion of the day's rations.

2.DETAILS RE-TURNING FROM THE LINE. Any details sent down from the line will report to Capt. H.H.WILKINSON at the wagon lines.

3.FIELD KITCHENS. Four Field Cookers will proceed to the CANAL BANK at [illegible] a.m. tomorrow. Dinners will be issued from the cookers at 12 mid-day. Tea will be prepared and issued at [illegible] p.m.

"A" & "B" Coys cookers will remain at the Canal Bank under Sergt. [illegible], where tea will be prepared and sent up the line in accordance with para:-

"C" Coy's cooker will proceed to [illegible] CAMP to cook for details, and "D" Coy's to the WAGON LINES.

4.DISTRIBUTION OF RATIONS. Each man carries TWO days' rations going in to the line. The rations for the further two days will be sent up and distributed as under:-

One limber containing TWO days' rations will leave the WAGON LINES at [illegible] p.m. on the [illegible]th, and proceed to [illegible] FARM, where the rations for two days will be dumped.

"D" Coy will distribute their SECOND days rations before proceeding to the front line.

The relieving Coy will distribute rations as soon as they have been relieved by "B" Coy and taken over the position at [illegible] FARM.

A Second Limber with TWO days' rations will proceed to [illegible] at [illegible] p.m. on the [illegible]th inst, and TWO days' rations will be dumped here and distributed in the same way as the other days.

Os.C., "A" & "B" Coys will be responsible for unloading the limbers on arrival at their respective Headquarters.

Coy.Q.M.Sergts. of "B" & "D" Coys will proceed to [illegible] FARM with "B" Coy tomorrow for the purpose of reconnoitring the way.

Coy.Q.M.Sergts. of "A" & "C" Coys will proceed to [illegible] with "A" Coy tomorrow for the same purpose.

All Coy.Q.M.Sergts. will return to the [illegible] as soon as they have ascertained the position of the Companies.

P.T.O.

COPY NO.......   TO BE DESTROYED WHEN COMPLIED WITH.

SECRET.

OPERATION ORDER No.4.
BY
LIEUT.COL.,E.V.MANGER,COMMANDING,
"K" BATTALION.

IN THE FIELD.   24th DECEMBER,1917.

(1) The Battalion will take over the LEFT Sub-Sector, HOUTHOUST FOREST from the Battalion holding the Line, in the following order:-

RIGHT COY:- "D" COY. (6 posts) H/QTRS:- Les 5 Chemins.

LEFT COY:- "C" COY. (6 posts) " By AJAX HOUSE.

SUPPORT COY:-"A" COY. " VEE BEND.
posts:-(2 platoons - Vee Bend.
(2 platoons - U.11. No.1.

RESERVE COY:-"B" COY. H/QTRS:- CRAONNE FARM.

Inter-Company Relief will take place on the night of the 27th/28th December.

(2) The Battalion will parade ready to march off at 9.30.a.m., and proceed to the CANAL BANK by Coys in file at 100 yards distance between Coys.
The Battalion will have dinner at the Canal Bank, and be ready to move at 2.30.p.m. via CLARGES STREET at 100 yards between platoons.

(3) On night of 24th/25th December a representative of each platoon will be sent into the front line system to ascertain the situation and assist the relief.
The two Officer representatives from 2 front line Coys will return to Canal Bank by 11.30.a.m. on the 25th, having ascertained the strength of each post, and the locality of each Lewis Gun other than anti-aircraft guns.

(4) GUIDES:- Guides for 2/9th K.L.R. will be sent to the Canal Bank by 1.0.p.m. on the 25th.
CLARGES STREET will be used for all 'up' traffic.

(5) Anti-aircraft Lewis Guns & Teams with anti-aircraft mountings, will be supplied by Coys at the following posts:-

"C" COY - AJAX HOUSE:- 1 Gun & Team.

"A" COY - U.17.a.5.9.) GRUYTERSZALE FARM) 2 Guns & 2 Teams.

"B" COY - MONT MORALL FARM:- 1 Gun & Team.

(6) S.O.S. POSTS will be taken over as follows:-
VEE BEND - One N.C.O. & 3 men from Battn Observers, and will be relieved with Companies.

(7) DRESS:- Leather Jerkins & Greatcoats will be worn - Haversacks on backs - 3 pairs of socks & 120 rounds of ammunition per man - two water bottles & two days' rations - Each man will be provided with a reserve ration of rum.
On Inter-Coy relief the returning Coys will take up two days' rations, and Coys relieved will have their rations dumped in the posts they take over. Each man in the front line Coys will carry and dump in his post 2 Mills' Bombs These will be handed over on Inter-Coy relief.

P.T.O.

(8) DEFENCE SCHEMES, AEROPLANE PHOTOS, MAPS, ETC, re: Brigade Sector will be taken over on relief - receipts in duplicate to be sent to Battn.H/Qtrs.

(9) RELIEF:-

will be reported to Battn.H/Qtrs by Fullerphone:-

"D" COMPANY.	-	"WILKIE"
"C" "	-	"MAIR"
"A" "	-	"MYERS"
"B" "	-	"LEE"

(10) EMILE CAMP to be left in a clean and sanitary condition. Os.C., Coys will render certificates to this effect by 8.30a.m. 25th inst.

@@@@@@@@@@@@@@@@@@

Lieut.Col.,
Commanding "K" Battaln.

Issued at...............

Copy No.1.	-	172nd Inf. Bde.
2.	-	2/8th K.L.R.
3.	-	2/5th S.L.R.
4.	-	C.O's File.
5.	-	Office File.
6.	-	"A" Coy.
7.	-	"B" "
8.	-	"C" "
9.	-	"D" "
10.	-	War Diary.

Confidential

12.8

172/57

W 12

War Diary

of

2/9th Battalion "The King's" (Liverpool) Regt.

From 1/1/1918. To 31/1/1918.

(Volume)

Instructions regarding War Diaries and Intelligence Summaries are contained in F. S. Regs., Part II. and the Staff Manual respectively. Title Pages will be prepared in manuscript.

WAR DIARY
or
INTELLIGENCE SUMMARY
(Erase heading not required.)

Army Form C. 2118

Place	Date	Hour	Summary of Events and Information	Remarks and references to Appendices
CANAL BANK BOESINGHE	1/1/18		One Company in the line attached to 2/4th Bn South Lancs Regt. Remainder of Battalion Working Parties.	[illegible]
	2/1/18		The Battalion less one company moved by Road & Rail from CANAL BANK to DYKES CAMP.	[illegible]
DYKES CAMP	3/1/18		Composite Company, attached to 2/4th Bn S. Lancs Regt in the line, rejoined at 2 am, having completed six days in the Front Line System. Hard frost continues. The physical condition of the men was good.	[illegible]
	4/1/18		The Battalion entrained at INTERNATIONAL CORNER at 10 am for BAILLEUL arriving at 1pm, and thence by road via STEENWERCK to WATERLANDS CAMP near ERQUINGHEM	[illegible]
WATERLANDS CAMP	5/1/18		Cleaning billets and Horse Lines, also Inspection of Kit.	[illegible]
	6/1/18		Divine Service. Inspection of Box Respirators	[illegible]
	7/1/18		Routine - Instructional Parades	[illegible]
	8/1/18		Observed as Christmas Day	[illegible]
	9/1/18		Instructional Parades. 2 Platoons Working under R.E Officers & Specialists reconnoitred the RIGHT EPINETTE SUB-SECTOR	[illegible]
	10/1/18		Physical Training under Brigade P.T Instructor. Platoon Commanders reconnoitred Front Line	[illegible]

1875 Wt. W593/826 1,000,000 4/15 J.B.C. & A. A.D.S.S./Forms/C. 2118.

Army Form C. 2118

Instructions regarding War Diaries and Intelligence Summaries are contained in F. S. Regs., Part II. and the Staff Manual respectively. Title Pages will be prepared in manuscript.

WAR DIARY
or
INTELLIGENCE SUMMARY
(Erase heading not required.)

Place	Date	Hour	Summary of Events and Information	Remarks and references to Appendices
WATERLANDS CAMP	11/1/18		ROUTINE. Close Order & Saluting Drill. Musketry and Bombing on Range. Battalion Bathed & received clean change of Clothing.	EBWR
	12/1/18		Preparation & Kit Inspections prior to going into the line	EBWR
L'EPINETTE SUB-SECTOR	13/1/18		The Battalion relieved the 2/8th Bn Liverpool Regt in the l'Epinette Sector	EBWR
	14/1/18		Very little hostile artillery fire. Machine Guns very active on Roads & Communication Trenches between 4-30 and 6 pm	EBWR
	15/1/18		A quiet day. A heavy fall of Snow and thaw following caused the earthworks and trenches to fall in, in many places. Constant working parties had to be employed keeping the Communication Trenches cleared and drained. The front posts and approaches to them were for the most part under water. Everything was done to try and improve the various posts but owing to the enormous amount of water it was impossible to effectively drain them.	EBWR Major 2/9th KLR

1875 Wt. W593/826 1,000,000 4/15 J.B.C. & A. A.D.S.S./Forms/C. 2118.

Army Form C. 2118

WAR DIARY
or
INTELLIGENCE SUMMARY
(Erase heading not required.)

Instructions regarding War Diaries and Intelligence Summaries are contained in F. S. Regs., Part II. and the Staff Manual respectively. Title Pages will be prepared in manuscript.

Place	Date	Hour	Summary of Events and Information	Remarks and references to Appendices
L'EPINETTE SUB. SECTOR	16/7/18		A quiet day. Machine Guns active at night. Heavy rain fell continuously making the condition of the trenches very bad. Work was continuously in progress on Communication Trenches & posts to keep them clear and as well drained as possible. During the night large quantities of wire was carried up and laid round front & support posts.	[illegible]
	17/7/18		A quiet day. Rain fell continuously during the day. Work was carried out during the day on keeping trenches clear and repairing damage caused by shell fire	[illegible]

1875 Wt. W593/826 1,000,000 4/15 J.B.C. & A. A.D.S.S./Forms/C. 2118.

Instructions regarding War Diaries and Intelligence Summaries are contained in F. S. Regs., Part II. and the Staff Manual respectively. Title Pages will be prepared in manuscript.

WAR DIARY
or
INTELLIGENCE SUMMARY
(Erase heading not required.)

Army Form C. 2118

Place	Date	Hour	Summary of Events and Information	Remarks and references to Appendices
L'EPINETTE SUB-SECTOR	17/1/18		During the night the wiring in of all posts was completed. Clean Socks were received for the first time during the tour in, although Socks were applied for on the 15th & 16th but were unobtainable	[signature]
	18/1/18		A quiet day. The Bn was relieved at 11pm by the 2/4th Bn South Lancs Regt. and came back to ARMENTIERES to act as Reserve Bn of Brigade in the line	[signature]
ARMENTIERES	19/1/18		Overland routes to Subsidiary Line reconnoitred by Officers & NCOs. Companies paraded for Cleaning, kit inspections & feet rubbing.	[signature] Major 2/9th KLR

1875 Wt. W593/826 1,000,000 4/15 J.B.C. & A. A.D.S.S./Forms/C. 2118.

Instructions regarding War Diaries and Intelligence Summaries are contained in F. S. Regs., Part II. and the Staff Manual respectively. Title Pages will be prepared in manuscript.

WAR DIARY
or
INTELLIGENCE SUMMARY
(Erase heading not required.)

Army Form C. 2118

Place	Date	Hour	Summary of Events and Information	Remarks and references to Appendices
ARMENTIERES,	20/1/18		Companies employed on working parties – wiring of posts & Right Flank of L'Ermitte Subsector	[illegible]
	21/1/18		Companies employed on working parties. The battalion was relieved at 6 pm by the 2/7th Bn Liverpool Regt and proceeded to WATERLANDS CAMP	[illegible]
WATERLANDS	22/1/18		One company Working Party, remainder of Battn Kit Inspection	[illegible]
	23/1/18		Working Parties all companies on ARMENTIERES DEFENCES	[illegible]
	24/1/18		Working Parties on ARMENTIERES DEFENCES	[illegible]
	25/1/18		Working Parties on ARMENTIERES DEFENCES. BATHS at PONT NIEPPE at disposal of Battalion	[illegible]
	26/1/18		Working Parties ARMENTIERES DEFENCES	[illegible]
	27/1/18		WORKING Parties. Church Parade. Battn relieved 2/6th Bn Kings Liverpool Regt as Battn in Brigade Reserve with Hdqrs in the CONVENT ARMENTIERES, three companies in the JUTE FACTORY & one in the ECOLE DES GARCONS. Relief complete at 8 pm	[illegible]

1875 Wt. W593/826 1,000,000 4/15 J.B.C. & A. A.D.S.S./Forms/C. 2118.

Instructions regarding War Diaries and Intelligence Summaries are contained in F. S. Regs., Part II. and the Staff Manual respectively. Title Pages will be prepared in manuscript.

WAR DIARY
or
INTELLIGENCE SUMMARY
(Erase heading not required.)

Army Form C. 2118

Place	Date	Hour	Summary of Events and Information	Remarks and references to Appendices
ARMENTIERES	28/1/18		Working Parties on TOWN DEFENCES night & day.	[illegible initials]
	29/1/18		Working Parties on TOWN DEFENCES night & day. A special Patrol of 1 NCO & 8 men under Lt L H COCKRAM went out from the Right Coy Sector of L'EPPINETTE Sub-sector to examine Enemy Wire at 5-15 pm. Whilst the work of examination was in progress, one of the enemy was noticed coming over the Parapet & making his way towards a gap in the wire. The Patrol lay low until the BOSCHE was within a few yards of them & they then captured him & returned to our lines. Although there was a number of the enemy in his front line, not a shot was fired. The Prisoner thus captured was a Corporal of the 131st I.R lately come over from Russia & was wearing the Decoration of the Iron Cross (2nd Class)	[illegible initials]
L'EPINNETTE SUB-SECTOR	30/1/18		The Battn relieved 2/4th Bn South Lancs Regt in the L'EPINNETTE SUB-SECTOR, relief being complete at 8/30pm. One Coy of the 2/4th Bn South Lancs attached for duty owing to this Battn being reduced in numbers. At 9-45 pm a Barrage was put down on Enemy Front & Support Lines opposite to the left Company Sector, and Dummy Figures were shown on our Parapet in order to give the Enemy an impression that a Raid was in progress. Owing to a heavy Ground mist it is almost certain that these figures could not be seen by the Enemy. Retaliation was only slight, in fact there was none at all until about 8 mins after our Barrage started. The Barrage lasted until 10-5 pm All quiet after about 10-30 pm.	[illegible signature] Major 2/9th [illegible]

1875 Wt. W593/826 1,000,000 4/15 J.B.C. & A. A.D.S.S./Forms/C. 2118.

Army Form C. 2118

Instructions regarding War Diaries and Intelligence Summaries are contained in F. S. Regs., Part II. and the Staff Manual respectively. Title Pages will be prepared in manuscript.

WAR DIARY
or
INTELLIGENCE SUMMARY
(Erase heading not required.)

Place	Date	Hour	Summary of Events and Information	Remarks and references to Appendices
L'EPINNETTE SUBSECTOR	31/1/18		A Quiet Day. Intermittent Machine Gun Fire at night.	[illegible] Major 2/9th KLR

1875 Wt. W593/826 1,000,000 4/15 J.B.C. & A. A.D.S.S./Forms/C. 2118.

57TH DIVISION
172ND INFY BDE

2-10TH KING'S L'POOLS
1915 AUG — 1916 FEB
AND FEB 1917 - ~~APR 1918~~
JULY 1918

Absorbed by 10 Bn. 1918 APL
See 55 DIV

www.ingramcontent.com/pod-product-compliance
Lightning Source LLC
Chambersburg PA
CBHW081441160426
43193CB00013B/2351

* 9 7 8 1 4 7 4 5 3 0 7 0 5 *